Parliamentary All-Party Penal Affairs Group

Young Offenders – A Strategy for the Future

July 1981

Previous report of the Parliamentary All-Party Penal Affairs Group:

Too Many Prisoners (1980)

© Parliamentary All-Party Penal Affairs Group

SBN 0 85992 225 1

Published by
Barry Rose (Publishers) Ltd
Chichester and London

Contents

P₅. 38 ·

CHAIRMAN'S FOREWORD

I wish to place on record our thanks to all the organisations and individuals who submitted evidence to us in the course of our enquiry. We set ourselves a relatively short period within which to complete our report. As a result, the pressure placed on those requested to submit evidence at short notice was considerable. Nevertheless, all responded in time and with valuable and informative submissions. That is a tribute to their commitment and efficiency which should not go unrecorded and for which we are grateful.

Our sincere thanks are also due to Paul Cavadino who, once again, coped with the difficult and time-consuming task of acting as secretary to the working party, the members of which repeatedly required the provision of more facts, more information or more evidence, and always at short notice. This report could not have been prepared without his generous and unfailing help.

Robert Kilroy-Silk
18 June 1981

YOUNG OFFENDERS – A STRATEGY FOR THE FUTURE

I: INTRODUCTION

1. "The extent to which a particular child may commit offences which go seriously beyond mischief depends on social deprivation (bad housing, poverty, poor schooling, broken families) more than any other factor", the House of Commons Expenditure Committee stated in 1975 in its report on the Children and Young Persons Act 1969. Many young offenders come from homes in which the parents are at odds or which are broken by desertion, separation and divorce, where parental discipline is lax, harsh or erratic, and where there is little encouragement for children to spend time with their parents or to organise their leisure time constructively – all of which underlines the importance of work with the families of delinquents in addition to measures which are concerned with young offenders themselves. While we consider that the considerable amount of disturbed and delinquent behaviour which occurs among the children of middle and upper income families is insufficiently acknowledged, it nevertheless remains true that a great deal of juvenile and young adult crime takes place in areas afflicted by a wide variety of social problems including poverty, high unemployment rates, poor housing conditions and a neglected and decaying environment. It is against this background that the present patterns of juvenile and young adult crime must be considered.

2. The main features of these patterns are as follows. First, the rate of recorded crime among juveniles (i.e. those under 17) is very much higher than for any other age group: in 1979 the rate was 6,810 indictable and triable-either-way offences* per 100,000 boys aged 14 and under 17 and 1,457 per 100,000 girls in this age group. In comparison, the figures for those aged 21 and over were 1,169 for males and 253 for females. The peak age for those found guilty or cautioned is 15 for boys and 14 for girls.

3. Thereafter, the proportions decline steadily, indicating that most young offenders leave delinquency behind them as they grow older. As the Black Report on legislation and services for children and young persons in Northern Ireland (1979) observed:

> "Fortunately for the community the minor nature of most juvenile crime is marked by its transience. We have already seen that most children and young people contravene the law in some way as they grow up. Many never come into contact with the police or other agencies. Most, however, do not persist in crime. Likewise, as far as we can tell, only a minority amongst juveniles who are prosecuted persist beyond a first or second

---

* "Indictable" offences are those triable only on indictment. "Triable either way" offences are triable either on indictment or summarily, but are triable summarily only with the consent of the accused.

1

offence. The indications are that many juvenile offenders, detected and undetected, mature out of that delinquency" (para. 5.28).

4.   Secondly, there has been a sharp rise over the years in the rate of recorded crime among young people. Over the last twenty years, the rate of crime per 100,000 young males has more than doubled, both in the case of juveniles and young adults (those aged 17 and under 21). Although the crime rate for females remains much lower than for males, the *increase* in crime among young women has been much sharper over the last two decades, during which time it has risen more than fourfold.

5.   Within the overall increase in crime rates among young people, there have, however, been considerable variations from year to year. For example, in 1975 and 1976 the rate of crimes committed by boys under 17 fell and, although it rose again in 1977, further falls occurred in 1978 and 1979. The level of crime among those aged 17 and under 21 has also fluctuated considerably, and in 1979 the crime rate among this age group (at 6,234 per 100,000 males and 925 per 100,000 females) fell to its lowest level since 1974.

6.   Thirdly, contrary to popular supposition, none of these trends appears to have been significantly affected by changes in the criminal law over the period, the most important of which was the passing of the Children and Young Persons Act 1969. There is no statistical evidence that the introduction of the Act and its implementation in 1971 affected juvenile offending. For one thing, there have been similar increases in both juvenile and adult crime over the last 20 years, although there has been no comparable legislation concerning young adult offenders. For another, the rise in juvenile crime showed a steady trend from 1967 till 1974, and there was no apparent change in this trend associated with the implementation of the 1969 Act in 1971.

7.   Fourthly, the bulk of the crime committed by young people does not involve violence. Most young offenders convicted and cautioned for indictable and triable-either-way offences have committed offences of theft and handling stolen goods, and the second largest offence group is burglary. A small proportion (8 per cent of juveniles and 16 per cent of young adults) have committed offences involving violence, sex or robbery. It remains the case, however, that offenders under 21 account for 46 per cent of all violent crime.

8.   Fifth, the overwhelming weight of evidence from research and of professional and other informed opinion now favours a major shift away from custodial measures and towards community-based methods of dealing with the vast majority of young offenders. Thus, the Expenditure Committee in its report of 1975 strongly recommended "a major shift of emphasis away from custodial and punitive techniques and towards intermediate schemes, supervision and a greater use of non-residential care" (para. 167). Similarly, the Advisory Council on the Penal System in its report "Young Adult Offenders" (1974) recommended "a major switch from custody to supervision in the community" for the young adult age group.

9.   The principal reason for this view was succinctly expressed by Mr Leon Brittan Q.C., M.P., then Minister of State at the Home Office, in a speech in Derby on 16 November 1979:

2

" . . . our aim must be to teach the young offender to live freely in the community without indulging in unacceptable behaviour. And it is obvious, from common sense, from experience and from research, that teaching anyone to come to terms with the community in which he lives must for the most part be better done in that community than in an artificial institutional setting providing supports which will be removed as soon as the youngster returns to his own home."

10. Yet (and this is the most disquieting fact of all), recent trends in the sentencing of young offenders have been precisely the reverse of this enlightened approach. While the percentage of juveniles given conditional discharges and fines is similar to that of a decade ago (and this accounts for the majority of juveniles sentenced for indictable offences and offences triable either way), the courts have used less and less the orders made available to them by the 1969 Children and Young Persons Act, i.e. care orders and supervision orders. There has instead been a sharp increase in the number and proportion of young offenders sent to detention centres, borstals and attendance centres.

11. The White Paper "Young Offenders" (1980)* describes the increase in custodial disposals as "one of the most disturbing aspects of the statistics for offending by and sentencing of juveniles during the past fifteen years" (para. 39). The number of juveniles committed to borstals and detention centres rose from 3,046 in 1969 to 7,161 in 1979, while over 5,000 fewer supervision orders were made in 1979 than probation orders on juveniles in 1969 — 16,229 as opposed to 21,652. In percentage terms the proportion of boys aged 14-16 convicted of indictable or triable-either-way offences who received custodial sentences increased from 6 per cent to 12 per cent over the decade, while the proportion receiving supervision orders fell from 23 per cent to 16 per cent for boys and from 32 per cent to 25 per cent for girls. (In 1979 there was a slight increase in the number of supervision orders and a drop in the number of custodial sentences imposed on juvenile offenders. While this is encouraging, the trend over the decade as a whole is an alarming one).

12. While there has not been an increase in the proportionate use of custody for the young adult age group, there has been little progress towards the major switch from custody to supervision in the community envisaged by the Advisory Council on the Penal System. Over half the young adults convicted of indictable or triable-either-way offences are fined. While the proportion receiving borstal and detention centre sentences has declined in the last ten years from 16 per cent to 12 per cent for males and from 3 per cent to 2 per cent for females, this has been largely counter-balanced numerically by an increase in the proportion receiving sentences of immediate imprisonment from 3 per cent to 6 per cent of males and from 1 per cent to 2 per cent of females in this age group. There has also been a marked decrease in the proportionate use of probation orders, from 14 per cent to 7 per cent in the case of young adult males and from 32 per cent to 18 per cent for young adult females (though for males this has been offset

---

* Hereafter, all allusions in this report to "the White Paper" refer to the White Paper, "Young Offenders", unless otherwise indicated.

numerically by a rapid increase in the use of community service orders in the last few years).

13. Overall, therefore, there has been a marked decline in the use of supervision in the community and, for the under seventeen age group, there has been a rapid and alarming rise in the use of custodial measures. Not only has the problem become worse over the last twenty years: the experience accumulated during that period suggests that the current trends in dealing with it are unlikely to improve it. Further details of trends in crime rates and sentencing patterns are contained in Appendices I and II.

14. In this report, we consider methods of dealing with offenders under 21 who have come to the notice of the police or courts. Thereafter, we intend to undertake an examination of a range of wider issues relating to crime among young people with a view to producing a further report in due course on preventive measures among this age group. In the chapters which follow, we consider possible methods of dealing with young offenders in ascending order of severity, beginning with diversion from the criminal justice system and thereafter examining community-based measures including fostering, intermediate treatment, attendance centres, fines, community service, restitution schemes and probation "packages"; care orders, including proposals for residential care orders and the use of secure accommodation; and finally custodial measures of various kinds.

15. Our general view is that the least restrictive appropriate disposition for each young offender should normally be used. We hope to demonstrate that, far from constituting a weak or ineffective response to crime among the young, this approach is more likely than any other to provide a rational and effective reaction to offending by children and young adults.

4

labelling

16. We endorse the view of the <u>Black Committee</u> that the prosecution of young offenders should be avoided "so far as is compatible with the protection of the public and the rights of the offender". As the White Paper points out, all the available evidence suggests that juvenile offenders who can be diverted from the criminal justice system at an early stage in their offending are less likely to re-offend than those who become involved in judicial proceedings. Similarly, the Black Committee, while accepting that the stigma attached to a court appearance may have a deterrent effect for some, pointed out that for other children who are convicted, the experience

> "is often a significant step in their delinquent career, confirming them in, rather than turning them from, further delinquent activity. Once labelled a delinquent, a child is more likely to see himself as such, to associate with kindred spirits, to be a focus of attention for the police, to become stereotyped. It is now widely accepted that conviction can have the effect of increasing, rather than diminishing, juvenile criminality" (para. 5.29).

We therefore consider that diversion from the criminal justice system should play a major role in society's response to young minor offenders in the early stages of offending.

Cautioning

17. We strongly support the system of administering formal police cautions, the use of which has increased markedly over the last twenty years for offenders under 17, so that most first time juvenile offenders who come to police notice are now cautioned. For a caution to be administered to a juvenile, the police must be satisfied that an offence was committed by the juvenile; the juvenile must admit the offence and that he knew it was wrong; and the parent or guardian must consent to the juvenile's being cautioned. The caution is usually administered in a formal way, to bring home the gravity of the occasion. An appointment will be made for the juvenile, with his parents, to attend at a police station where he will be seen by a senior officer in uniform, who administers the caution.

18. The Black Committee rightly stressed that the cautioning of young offenders is not a soft option: rather it is a positive response to delinquency, which aims to help and encourage children to channel their energy and desires into legitimate activities. It identified four factors contributing to this aim. First, if correctly identified, the child involved is by definition not a persistent delinquent and might well, like many others not detected, mature out of the offending phase. Second, the police warning should have an impact on the child, making him think of the consequences before reoffending. Third, the warning should alert the child's family, who may not previously have been aware of his

activities or of the company he keeps. This should increase the prospects of their exerting a positive influence on him. Finally, notification to the helping agencies should result in efforts to deal with any negative factors in the child's life.

19. Cautioning has a high success rate: for example, of 9,000 first time juvenile offenders cautioned by the Metropolitan Police in 1976, only 20 per cent had come to police notice again by April 1978. Smaller sample studies in other police areas have produced similar findings.

Variations in cautioning rates
20. There is considerable variation in cautioning rates from area to area: the proportion of boys under 17 convicted or cautioned for indictable or triable — either-way offences who were cautioned in 1978 varied from 34 per cent in Humberside to 67 per cent in Essex, and in 1979 from 28 per cent in South Wales to 67 per cent in Dyfed-Powys. Cautioning rates for burglary vary from 16% to 59%, for theft from 35% to 74% and for summary offences (excluding motoring offences) from 5% to 67%. More detailed figures of cautioning rates in different parts of the country and for different types of offence are contained in Appendix III.

21. Even in the high-cautioning area of Essex, David Thorpe, Christopher Green and David Smith of Lancaster University found that 58 per cent of 131 young offenders appearing before the juvenile court in Basildon had never previously been cautioned. In their research study, "Punishment and Welfare" (University of Lancaster, 1979), they pointed out that this raises questions about the extent to which cautioning is being used as a diversionary mechanism and about the criteria that the police use in considering a child for a caution:

> "If over 50% of children appearing before the court do so without ever having been cautioned, then it seems clear that it is not being used as it was originally intended, i.e. to deal with children's first offences in a less formal and stigmatising manner."

Twenty of these cases (16 per cent) resulted in absolute or conditional discharges, which suggests that a considerable number of these cases need not have been brought before a court. Similarly, in the authors' analysis of young offenders given care orders in Rochdale, just over half had been prosecuted rather than cautioned for their first offence and 75 per cent had been prosecuted for their second offence.

22. The Magistrates' Association has frequently expressed its concern regarding inconsistencies in the administration of police cautions and the Justices' Clerks' Society, in its "Recommendations for Child Law Reform" (May 1980) commented that cautioning is administered by the police in a "haphazard and unjust way". The Society proposed that police cautioning should be abolished and replaced by a new power for the courts after finding a case proved to dismiss the juvenile with a warning or admonition which is not legally a finding of guilt. However, this proposal seems to have no support from the other organisations which have submitted evidence to us: they are generally in favour of the cautioning system, though worried about inconsistencies in its application.

23. The Association of Chief Police Officers put three arguments to us against

the Justices' Clerks' Society's proposal. First, it pointed out that criticisms of inconsistency in the administration of cautions on the basis of statistical variations are similar to criticisms which are frequently levelled at the court system. Secondly, it expressed scepticism concerning the juvenile courts' ability to take on the additional burden of those at present cautioned without a significant increase in the number of courts and court staff. Finally, it observed that the appearance of such juveniles before the court "would be totally against the spirit of the 1969 Act, which attempted to reduce, as far as possible, the stigma of juveniles appearing before a court".

24. The Police Superintendents' Association has suggested to us that variations in cautioning rates may represent "a considerable variation in crimes and criminals" rather than any variation in police practice. Similarly, the Association of Chief Police Officers pointed out that the cautioning rate is higher in the predominantly rural counties than for urban and metropolitan areas, and suggested that this reflected "the problems of policing densely populated areas where the crime rate is high and the social/environmental facilities limited within particular communities". While accepting that there is a subjective element in decisions and that "inevitably there will be local variations", the Association commented that there are a number of factors outside police officers' control which may affect cautioning rates — for example, the availability of resources such as intermediate treatment, which may dispose more favourably to administering a caution.

25. The report of the Royal Commission on Criminal Procedure (1981), while acknowledging that some of the variations were "explicable in terms of the area which the forces are required to police" (para. 6.41), concluded that there were clearly different force policies in this matter and drew attention to "the scope for increasing consistency of police practice in regard to the decision to caution as an alternative to prosecution". Observing that the formal police caution has at present no firm statutory basis, the Royal Commission suggested that "the time has come for the use of the formal caution to be sanctioned in legislation and put on a more consistent basis" (para. 7.59). **We recommend that the use of the caution should be sanctioned in legislation and attention should be given to achieving greater consistency throughout the country.**

26. We are attracted by the Black Committee's proposal that all first or second minor offenders who admit guilt should be cautioned by the police and that only "cases which pose a real or serious threat to society" should go before the juvenile court. **We recommend that all first-time minor offenders under seventeen who admit guilt should be cautioned, and this should also be the normal practice in regard to those who commit a second minor offence.**

Cautioning as an alternative to prosecution
27. It seems that cautioning is not always used as alternative to prosecution, but is sometimes used for young offenders in whose case no prosecution would otherwise be brought. Home Office Research Study No. 37, "Police Cautioning in England and Wales" (1976), concluded:

". . . there seems little doubt that increased cautioning has diverted substantial numbers of juvenile offenders from court appearances".

28. It nevertheless identified two features which suggested that increased cautioning may have had an "inflationary" as well as a diversionary effect. First, taking the police forces of England and Wales as a whole, there has been a close connection between the growth of juvenile cautioning since 1968 and increases in the known offender rate for juveniles. In general, those areas which had made the greatest use of cautioning had also recorded the largest increases in the number of known offenders. Secondly, some areas that had increased cautioning on a large scale had also shown large increases in the ratio of juveniles to adults in the offender population.

29. David Steer's study "Police Cautions — a study in the exercise of police discretion" (1970) provides further evidence that in a significant number of cases cautions are administered where no prosecution would otherwise have been brought. Of the samples he examined, cautions were administered in 20% of the cases where there was insufficient evidence for prosecution, one force cautioning in 5% of such cases and another force cautioning in 31%. Cautions were also administered in a further 20% of cases where the complainant was unwilling to give evidence in a prosecution. Detective Chief Inspector Donald Taylor of the Avon and Somerset Constabulary, writing recently in "Justice of the Peace" (10th May 1980), argued that

> ". . . a formal recorded caution is not appropriate in such cases. Strong advice may be expedient and indeed sensible, but in order that the recipients are not left with a sense of injustice, such cautions should not be a matter of record."

The practice of citing official police cautions when giving a juvenile's antecedent history in court lends strength to this argument, which we endorse. **We recommend that formal cautions should not be administered where there is insufficient evidence for prosecution.**

Cautioning of young adults

30. The proportion of young adult offenders cautioned for indictable or triable-either-way offences is very low in comparison with the figures for juveniles: the percentages in 1979 were 3 per cent for males and 5 per cent for females in this age group. In our earlier report "Too Many Prisoners" (1980), we recommended that the use of police cautioning for adult offenders should be extended, and we consider that this recommendation is equally applicable to young adults. **We recommend that cautioning should be used more often for young adult offenders.**

An independent prosecutor

31. The greater consistency which we favour in decisions to prosecute or to caution could more readily be achieved within the framework of an independent prosecutor system. In its evidence to us, the National Association of Probation Officers said that it had been impressed by its recent research into the Dutch criminal justice system, in particular the practice of the independent prosecutor who often discharges as many as 50 per cent of the charges which come before him, on the grounds that it would not necessarily be in the public interest to proceed with the case. The Association commented:

> "There is an increasing feeling among those of us that work very closely

with the courts that there is an unacceptably high rate of very trivial offences being brought before the magistrates' courts".

32. Our attention has also been drawn to the practice in Scotland, where the reporter to the children's panel receives referrals from the police and other agencies and individuals of children who are believed to be "in need of compulsory measures of care", including those who have committed offences. (A child may be dealt with in the sheriff court or High Court rather than referred to the reporter if he is alleged to have committed a serious offence such as murder, rape or serious assault or if the offence also involved an adult). Following the referral, the reporter has unfettered discretion in deciding what steps to take. He may decide to take no further action, and does so with half the offences referred to him. He may arrange for voluntary supervision of the child by the local authority social work department or refer the child back to the police for a formal warning, but this happens in only a minority of cases: four fifths of the offence cases diverted from children's hearings are not brought to the notice of any agency. Alternatively, he may bring the child before a children's hearing. In making their decisions, reporters acquire information from social work, school and other sources, and their decisions to divert are in practice influenced by a combination of known prior record, seriousness of current offence and awareness of problems in the domestic background. As a result of the operation of this system, the total number of appearances by juveniles before children's hearings and courts in Scotland is now less than half the number proceeded against in the various courts ten years ago.

33. A third model is the proposal of the Royal Commission on Criminal Procedure that a statutorily based prosecution service should be established for every police force area in England and Wales. This would conduct all criminal cases once the decision to initiate proceedings has been taken by the police, and after that point the prosecution service would have complete discretion to alter or drop charges.

34. We have not undertaken a detailed examination of the respective merits of different systems which involve separation of the functions of investigation and prosecution. It is nevertheless clear that consistency in decisions between prosecution and cautioning could more readily be attained within such a system, and this is true in relation both to young offenders and to adult offenders. **We recommend that the function of prosecution should be performed by a service independent of the service responsible for the investigation of offences.**

Summary of recommendations
1. The use of the caution should be sanctioned in legislation and attention should be given to achieving greater consistency in cautioning practice throughout the country (para. 25).

2. All first-time minor offenders under seventeen who admit guilt should be cautioned, and this should also be the normal practice in regard to those who commit a second minor offence (para. 26).

3. Formal cautions should not be administered where there is insufficient evidence for prosecution (para. 29).

4. Cautioning should be used more often for young adult offenders (para. 30).

5. The function of prosecution should be performed by a service independent of the service responsible for the investigation of offences (para. 34).

35. In a speech to the Centre of Youth, Crime and Community at Lancaster University on 18th September 1980, the Home Secretary stated that

"The Government is committed to seeing all offenders, of whatever age, dealt with in the community wherever possible . . . because we believe that no-one should be deprived of his liberty unless that is absolutely unavoidable".

We strongly support this approach, which depends for its success on the provision in all areas of the country of a range of community-based alternatives to custody and residential care. In some cases, the activities and obligations inherent in these alternative measures may be made explicit in a court order; in others they will be used at the discretion of supervising probation officers or social workers. While the promotion of such alternatives is the responsibility of central and local government, it is important that individual members of the community should be encouraged to take part in statutory schemes on a voluntary basis and that statutory support should be given to schemes run by voluntary organisations which provide credible alternatives to custodial and residential establishments.

Professional fostering schemes

36. We have been greatly impressed by the operation of the "family placement" and "professional fostering" schemes which have been established by an increasing number of local authorities over the last few years. These aim to provide a family environment for difficult or delinquent teenagers who are in the care of the local authority and who are unable to live at home. Although in the past social services departments have found it hard to find foster parents prepared to take on older children (14-17 year olds being the hardest of all), particularly those with a history of delinquency, a number of authorities are now meeting with considerable success in recruiting suitable foster parents for their professional fostering schemes.

37. There are now about thirty such schemes operating throughout the United Kingdom, and the preliminary findings indicate that placement in a family is beneficial for many teenagers, giving them the guidance, help, affection and discipline which they need and setting the limits which make life bearable in any family. Several schemes are intended for teenagers who would otherwise have gone to community homes with education (and in some cases to detention centres and borstals) and such placements provide a preferable alternative to residential care or custody for many whose removal from home is considered essential.

38. Families in such schemes are normally paid a professional weekly fee for

their work in addition to the normal fostering allowances. Parents in such schemes have often had some kind of related experience in social work, teaching, psychiatric nursing or some other relevant discipline. However, this is by no means the case with all such parents, and the progress report on the Wakefield scheme published in December 1979 expresses a widely held view:

> "Although feeling that experience in social work, teaching or nursing might be helpful, we have never insisted on this. Experience has proved that ordinary families can undertake this task provided they possess the right personal qualities, among which one can list a sense of humour, resilience, flexibility, the ability to look at themselves objectively and to have others look at them, and above all commitment".

39. The Kent Family Project, which was set up in 1975, has been particularly well documented, and a number of subsequent schemes have explicitly modelled themselves on Kent. Teenagers selected for the Kent project must be aged 14 to 17, in the care of the local authority, with severe problems and willing to take part in the project. They may come from a residential establishment or from their own home. A high percentage of referrals have come from residential establishments and the project has in almost all cases taken teenagers who would otherwise have gone into residential care. The project normally rejects cases which are ineligible under its terms of reference (e.g. no severe problems, too young, mentally handicapped or with a history of arson) but otherwise attempts to place any case which is referred. A temporary halt is called if the number of referrals exceeds the project's available manpower. From the beginning of the scheme to 31 December 1979, 179 teenagers were placed with families: 75 were in placement on 31 December 1979. The majority of those placed by the project have been through the courts on at least one occasion.

40. The principle of payment is that the families are being paid fees for difficult and skilled jobs. Families are paid a professional fee, currently £57.23 per week. In addition a non-taxable boarding-out rate is paid, which at present (including clothing allowance and pocket money) is £23.50 per week for a 15 year old and £26.50 for a 16 year old. In many cases the wife has a career, which she may have given up while her children are young but to which she might expect to return later. The professional fee must therefore be sufficiently high to compete with alternative sources of income such as part time teaching.

41. The project aims to help the teenagers either to return to their own homes after a specified period of time or, with the help of the foster family, to launch themselves into independent living. Either way, the foster parents are expected to work closely with the family of origin so that, even if the adolescent does not wish to return to his own home, he can leave as a normal young adult, having established a satisfactory visiting relationship wherever possible. In most cases parents agree to the placement and are keen to meet the prospective foster parents. The idea of a time-limited and problem-solving placement as a bridge towards the adolescent's adult life tends to be less threatening and more acceptable to the child's own parents than a traditional fostering placement. Moreover, parents often feel that a placement of this kind is preferable to and more constructive than a residential establishment, as do the teenagers themselves.

42. The placements are based on a written contract between the family, the teenager, the project and the social worker which tries to specify the tasks to be undertaken. All agreements are reviewed and may be amended at either three or six monthly intervals, when the placement is evaluated. The contracts for the adolescent and the foster family will specify the intended length of the placement and the procedure for ending it, the adolescent's role in the family, the specific problems to be tackled, the intentions for school or work and the arrangements for contact with the family of origin. The family of origin are asked to commit themselves to various tasks, depending on the aims of the placement and the needs and wishes of the child. For example, they may agree to have the child home for a weekend every month or to write to him every week.

43. Support for foster parents is crucial to the project's successful operation. Each project officer is responsible for supervising and supporting 12 to 15 foster parents and a maximum of 20 children, a high staff/foster parent ratio. Furthermore, foster parents support themselves through regular small group meetings. They help each other out in crises, discuss problems they are having with their placements, give advice to new or prospective foster parents and, in some cases, even transfer an adolescent to another member of the group if the placement breaks down (provided this is agreed by the project officer).

44. During the project's lifetime, its foster families have proved themselves able to give affectionate care and understanding, and have shown that they can cope with delinquent behaviour as well as emotional disturbance, whether overt or hysterical or taking the form of withdrawal. Dr Margaret Yelloly, Head of the Department of Applied Social Studies at Goldsmiths' College, London, has carried out an independent evaluation of 25 consecutive placements which Sir George Young M.P., Parliamentary Under-Secretary of State at the DHSS, referred to as "extremely encouraging" in a written Parliamentary answer of 11 December 1979. Almost two-thirds of the placements (64 per cent) were successful in that the placement was completed as planned, and 76 per cent of the adolescents were considered by the evaluator to have clearly benefited during the period of placement. Some modification of delinquent activities had occurred in half the young offenders placed. Dr Yelloly commented:

"Given the degree of social and emotional deprivation which these adolescents had experienced, a much more pessimistic conclusion might have been anticipated."

45. The project's fourth report, published in January 1980, states that of the first 156 teenagers placed, 111 (71 per cent) improved in placement. It adds:

"We seem to have developed a close relationship with the courts. Judges and magistrates are sometimes prepared to risk a family placement where borstal seemed a foregone conclusion."

46. The Director of Social Services for Kent has stressed to us the need to devote adequate resources to the establishment of such schemes. Nevertheless, it is estimated that the total cost of a family placement in the scheme (including the cost of support by social workers etc.) is about half that of a residential place for a "high problem" adolescent. On 1st January 1980 the project, which had previously had semi-autonomous status as a demonstration project, became

fully integrated into Kent Social Services Department.

47. In 1976 Wakefield Social Services Department established a professional fostering scheme, modelled on the Kent scheme. The aim is to use the scheme as an alternative to a community home with education for children aged between 12 and 18 who have come into care having committed offences and have associated emotional and behavioural problems which cannot be dealt with at home. The professional foster parents receive a fee of £41 per week plus boarding-out allowances. The professional fee is taxable but the local Inland Revenue has agreed that £11 per week may be off-set against expenses or the foster parents may, if they prefer, submit a detailed expense claim. Twenty-six children had been placed up to December 1979, when 15 families were involved in the scheme. Only one placement was considered to have broken down, though two others ended before the contracted time. Only one young person re-offended while in the foster home and two after leaving foster homes.

48. The Birmingham Special Family Placement Scheme began in the autumn of 1976 for juveniles presenting special difficulties that would otherwise have to be dealt with in a community home with education or a community home which specialises in dealing with more difficult children. The 18 foster families which participate in the scheme are paid a professional fee of £45 per week while a child is with them. 44 young people have been placed with the scheme's families: 15 of these had previous records of court appearances, four of whom have re-offended during their placements and a further one following placement. A large proportion of the remaining 29 children had a record of behaviour which placed them at high risk of prosecution, only one of whom has offended during a placement: one other child was convicted after finishing a placement.

49. The Bradford Community Parents Scheme began in the autumn of 1977, based on the Kent Project's methods, for young people aged 14-17, the majority of whom would otherwise be placed in community homes with education. 27 families are currently participating in the scheme in return for a professional fee of £41 during placement plus the normal boarding-out allowances. On 31 March 1980, there were 21 youngsters in placement. Of the 74 young people who have been placed with community parents, only eight have committed offences during placement leading to court appearances. None of the young people of working age have been unemployed for long periods while on the scheme and there has been little chronic non-school attendance. Follow-up surveys have found that most of those who have completed a placement and been away from their community parents for more than three months have subsequently maintained this level of progress, and there has been little subsequent re-offending.

50. Other areas with professional fostering schemes for difficult and delinquent adolescents include Bolton, Cheshire, Cornwall, Coventry, Cumbria, Derbyshire, Dorset, Hertfordshire, Humberside, Isle of Wight, Lambeth, Northamptonshire, Nottinghamshire, Oxfordshire, Reading, Surrey, Sutton and Westminster.

51. **We recommend that professional fostering schemes should be supported and extended, and the DHSS should give local authorities positive guidance and encouragement to develop such schemes.**

Intermediate treatment

52. The development of a wide range of intermediate treatment (I.T.) schemes should form a central part of policies towards juvenile offending. Intermediate treatment schemes aim to reduce delinquency by involving young people in constructive activities, offering them opportunities for achievement, improving their social skills, bringing them into contact with mature adults who can exercise a positive influence on them, providing counselling both individually and in groups, and involving the parents of delinquents in taking more responsibility for their children's behaviour. While most I.T. facilities are provided by local authorities, voluntary organisations also play an important part in the provision of I.T. and have been the spearhead of much innovatory practice. Many projects use individual volunteers who can relate well to youngsters and who have a skill to share, such as motor cycle maintenance, music or outward bound activity.

53. Many schemes are based on small groups meeting weekly with occasional short residential experiences. There is an increasing number of intermediate treatment centres, which act as a focus for activities for young offenders and those at risk, house group meetings and from which other activities in the community can be undertaken. Some centres provide more intensive I.T. on a daily basis for those offenders who are not in full time education or employment. A more detailed description of the operation of four intermediate treatment schemes is contained in Appendix IV.

54. Section 12(2) of the 1969 Children and Young Persons Act provided that a supervision order may require the supervised person to comply with the supervisor's directions to participate in approved activities. The term "intermediate treatment" is not, however, confined to participation in activities under this legislative provision but is also used to describe schemes catering for young people thought to be at risk of getting into trouble.

55. The National Youth Bureau estimates that during the year 1978/79 there were about 20-25,000 children involved in I.T. in England and Wales, of whom about 15 per cent were subject to supervision orders with an I.T. requirement. Over half were probably subject to a court order of some kind, usually a supervision order without an I.T. requirement, while a third or more were subject to no court order. The Bureau also estimates that in September 1979 there were about 650 people in Britain employed by statutory and voluntary agencies who were engaged more or less full time in some form of I.T. work, compared with 350 in January 1978. In addition, thousands of social workers, probation officers and volunteers were engaged in I.T. work for a limited number of hours a week. In mid-1979 there were 60 I.T. centres in England and Wales and an estimated 3,000 children were involved in programmes at these centres: since then the number of centres and the number of children involved has grown considerably. The cost of intermediate treatment programmes varies from £100 or less per child per year for the least intensive programmes to between £2,000 and £4,000 a year for the most intensive, compared with an average cost of £10,000 a year to maintain a child in a community home with education (1980/81 figures), £7,823 for a borstal place and £6,505 for a detention centre place (1979/80 figures).

56. Local authorities' estimated gross expenditure on intermediate treatment in England and Wales in 1980/81 was £6.1 million. However, this figure does not cover the full cost of I.T. provision because authorities differ greatly in what they classify as expenditure on I.T., and the total gross expenditure may actually amount to over £7 million. This is a fraction of the £85 million spent on running local authority community homes with education and observation and assessment centres.

57. As Sir George Young M.P., Parliamentary Under-Secretary at the DHSS, pointed out in an address to the Leicester Action for Youth Trust on 12 February 1981:

"At present the development of I.T. is too patchy. Some areas can boast a wide range of activities provided from a variety of sources; in others, almost no facilities are available. Everywhere, I.T. at the 'heavier' end — that is for youngsters convicted of more than just petty crimes and beyond the reach of many of the programmes — is very sparsely available".

58. We are concerned at the inconsistency of intermediate treatment provision and the serious lack of I.T. facilities in some areas. With isolated exceptions, few areas can claim to have developed a comprehensive range of I.T. schemes. Thus in 1980/81 the 10 per cent of local authorities with the highest I.T. budgets accounted for 38 per cent of the national total spent on such activities. 10 per cent of authorities spent £5,000 or less on I.T. — less than the annual cost of keeping one juvenile in a custodial or residential establishment.

59. The Secretary of State for Social Services, speaking in Sheffield on 9 July 1979, stated that

"the Government is prepared to regard child care services as an integral part of the national pattern of law and order services, and to have the priority which that accords it".

Despite the Government's wish that this area should be given such priority, the recent Social Priorities Alliance report, "Cuts in Local Authority Spending on Personal Social Services" (1980), found that at least nine authorities were reducing their provision for intermediate treatment and that 19 per cent of their detailed sample of authorities cut their I.T. budgets in 1979-80 and 6 per cent in 1980-81.

60. It is worrying that so few of those taking part in intermediate treatment appear to do so as a direct alternative to residential care or custody, and concern about this has been expressed by the Justices' Clerks' Society, the British Association of Social Workers and New Approaches to Juvenile Crime among others. Two examples of a constructive response to this concern are NACRO's DHSS-financed Community Alternatives for Young Offenders team, which is currently working with seven local authorities to develop intermediate treatment schemes for the more persistent or serious young offenders, and the Centre of Youth, Crime and Community at Lancaster University, which is assisting several local authorities to re-allocate resources from residential care to intermediate treatment.

61. **We recommend that there should be a range of intermediate treatment,**

catering both for young offenders and those at risk. Within this range, greater efforts should be made to provide intermediate treatment for juveniles who would otherwise have been committed to custodial and residential establishments.

62. At present, when a court makes a supervision order, it can confer substantial powers on the supervisor, including the power to direct attendance at I.T. facilities. However, it is for the supervisor to decide whether and to what extent he uses these powers and what facilities should be used. The White Paper comments that

> "generally, except where there is very close liaison the magistrates do not necessarily know what, if anything, will happen under the order. They might for that reason understandably hesitate to make a supervision order, particularly in the case of a serious or difficult offender" (para. 49).

63. The Magistrates' Association in its observations on the working of the Children and Young Persons Act (May 1980) proposed that legislation should be introduced to direct the child to undergo I.T. and the supervisor to ensure its execution. Similarly, the Justices' Clerks' Society in its recent paper on child law reform argued that magistrates should be empowered to insist that intermediate treatment is carried out or the defendant brought back to court within a period of, say, three months for variation of the order.

64. The Government proposed in the White Paper to give the court a specific power to order a juvenile offender under supervision to undertake a programme of specified activities which has been agreed between the supervising probation officer or social worker and the court as being suitable for that particular young person, and which the offender has agreed to undertake. The new order might be known as a supervised activities order or an intermediate treatment order. (We share the view that "intermediate treatment" is an unfortunate title and we have some sympathy for the proposed alternative title "supervised activities", though this in turn has the potential disadvantage that it may tend to under-value the role which counselling plays in many I.T. schemes). The Government argues that this power to determine broadly a suitable programme of activities, in the light of professional advice from the social worker or probation officer, will give the courts greater confidence in the supervision order and in the use of intermediate treatment.

65. In its comments on the White Paper, the Association of Directors of Social Services sought reassurance that the programme will not be too rigidly applied:

> "The I.T. plan agreed must be flexible, so that it may be amended in the light of the child's changing needs and circumstances, or to take advantage of new I.T. facilities which were not available when the order was made, without the necessity of going back to court."

The Association's proposals would leave it to the court to specify the duration of intermediate treatment and to the supervisor to choose the particular activities required of the young person. Similarly, the Conference of Chief Probation Officers argued in its comments on the White Paper that the order should not stipulate the actual activity to be carried out. As with community service orders, the court would indicate the general limits of the requirement "and it would be for the service, in communication with benches through case committees and in other ways, to give information about the detail of its projects and of the activities undertaken by individuals."

66. The main attraction of the Government's proposal for a new order is that the courts could be encouraged to use it specifically as an alternative to custody or residential care. However, the Magistrates' Association has told us that it favours making the present supervision order effective rather than introducing a new type of order and the Association of Directors of Social Services has proposed that the intermediate treatment contract should be included as a requirement of a supervision order and not as a separate kind of order, while the Association of Metropolitan Authorities has described the proposed new order as "superfluous".

67. Whichever approach is adopted, we recommend that, before imposing an intermediate treatment requirement, the court should satisfy itself that the programme envisaged by the social worker or probation officer is appropriate. We further recommend that intermediate treatment requirements should be mandatory and their implementation should not be left to the supervisor's discretion. However, discretion should be given to the supervising officer to modify the detailed content of the intermediate treatment programme in the light of changing circumstances.

68. No legislative provision for intermediate treatment can be effective unless it is supported by sufficient finance to develop a range of I.T. facilities in which the courts and supervising officers can have confidence. Several local authorities have reduced their use of residential establishments in order to develop community-based schemes. For example, the Director of Social Services for Essex told us that the closure of a community home with education in Chelmsford has saved the authority a gross sum of £400,000 per annum and that "closure provides a real incentive to look at alternative forms of care of a non-custodial nature".

We recommend that local authorities should be encouraged to transfer resources from residential care, to intermediate treatment. Residential care is, however, required for a minority of young people and we further recommend that this transfer should be achieved in a manner which ensures that the resulting smaller scale residential sector is adequately financed with a complement of well trained and highly valued staff.

69. The Government has indicated that it intends to add extra finance of the order of £1 million per annum to the rate support grant for the development of intermediate treatment. This amount compares unfavourably with the £5 million which will be required to finance the proposed residential care order. Moreover, since this finance will not be earmarked, local authorities will not be obliged to spend it in this way and will be free if they wish to divert it to other electorally more popular areas. We recommend that the extra finance intended for the development of intermediate treatment which is to be added to the rate support grant should be increased to a level at least comparable with the extra £5 million necessitated by the proposed residential care order. This should be combined

with a statutory requirement on local authorities to provide certain minimum levels of intermediate treatment. The attainment of these minimum levels would be subject to inspection by the Secretary of State for Social Services.

70. The Magistrates' Association proposed in its memorandum of May 1980 that Probation and After-Care Committees should also have budgetary control over funds allocated to I.T. and the White Paper proposed that probation and after-care committees should be enabled to provide intermediate treatment facilities "in a way which is consistent with proper co-ordination of local arrangements". In its comments on the White Paper, the Conference of Chief Probation Officers welcomed this proposal and stated:

> "We should want to grasp this opportunity wholeheartedly and to develop sentencing options which can effectively attract the confidence of the courts. This would clearly have financial implications which we would expect to be taken seriously".

71. However, the Association of Directors of Social Services in its comments on the White Paper, while welcoming the additional resources for I.T., argued that the finance should be given to local authorities for this purpose:

> "Youngsters supervised by probation officers have full access to all I.T. schemes run by local authorities and voluntary organisations. The development of a separate Probation I.T. Scheme would pose considerable problems for the future. Courts may be tempted to make increasing use of probation officers for the supervision of juveniles, at a time when the probation service is under pressure to meet the needs of its adult clientele".

72. We consider it far from satisfactory that in areas where probation officers are supervising the majority of juvenile offenders, the probation service should be completely dependent on the good will of another agency for finance for intermediate treatment schemes. Where the local authority is sympathetic to I.T. and relations between the agencies are good, no problems may arise, but in other areas local authorities have shown themselves unwilling to devote anything like adequate resources to I.T.

73. **We recommend that the probation service should be enabled to provide intermediate treatment facilities in a way which is consistent with proper co-ordination of local arrangements.**

74. Voluntary organisations have an important role to play in the development of a comprehensive range of intermediate treatment facilities and we endorse the Expenditure Committee's recommendation in 1975 that "both individuals and voluntary organisations be encouraged to co-operate in intermediate treatment". In the financial year 1980/81, the DHSS made £500,000 available in individual grants to voluntary organisations engaged in developing innovative I.T. schemes. In addition, since its establishment in 1978, successive Governments have supported the Rainer Foundation Intermediate Treatment Fund, which has provided capital grants to voluntary organisations and individuals willing to provide I.T. facilities which local authorities are prepared to use. The Fund is particularly concerned to support modest schemes which are low on cost but high on community involvement.

75. In the first two years of its operation, the Fund received £200,000 per annum from central government. During that period, 175 projects were helped by the Fund and the amount of grant aid given or approved in principle was £371,636. In addition, over £200,000 was contributed to I.T. schemes by private grant-making bodies as a direct result of the Fund's involvement. At the start of the financial year 1980-81, the DHSS made the Fund a grant of £223,000 which has recently been supplemented by an additional £50,000. In the year 1981-82, the Department has agreed to augment the Fund's basic grant of £240,000 by up to a further £150,000 in proportion to the financial involvement in the Fund's work of trusts and other outside bodies.

76. The Fund's annual report for 1979-80 commented:

> "Projects are experiencing increasing difficulty in finding resources to meet running costs, both statutory and private funding sources being more reserved currently about meeting these. Difficulty about finding money for salaries seems a main inhibitor to project expansion or initiation".

As the Fund's grants have hitherto been awarded for capital purposes only, they could not therefore be used for running costs. In its comments on the White Paper, the National Council for Voluntary Organisations proposed the creation of a new expanded intermediate treatment fund, combining the various monies spent on I.T. by central government and able to fund salary and revenue costs as well as capital costs. It has now been agreed that in future the Fund will consider applications from intermediate treatment projects for limited amounts of assistance with running costs in order to help initiate projects, but with the proviso that the local authority will assume financial support thereafter. While we welcome this development as a step in the righf direction, we consider that much more needs to be done. There is likely to be a very large number of applications from schemes seeking grants towards running costs, many of which the Fund will be unable to satisfy.

77. **We recommend that there should be increased central government funding for intermediate treatment schemes run by voluntary organisations, and in particular there should be a considerable further increase in the funds available to the Rainer Foundation Intermediate Treatment Fund. We further recommend that greater encouragement and support for voluntary initiatives in intermediate treatment should be provided by the statutory services.**

78. New Approaches to Juvenile Crime pointed out in its memorandum to the Secretary of State for Social Services and the Home Secretary of March 1980 that successive Governments have considered the provision of secure units in community homes with education to be of such importance that substantial central government funding has been made available to local authorities for this purpose. It argued that the provision of "heavy end" intermediate treatment schemes is of sufficient importance to merit a similar injection of central funding and proposed that

> ". . . such finance should be made available to social services departments, probation services or voluntary organisations which demonstrate that they have a viable proposed scheme which will cater for a substantial number of

juveniles who would otherwise be committed to residential or custodial establishments".

79. Precedents for the provision of central government funding for facilities managed by local authorities include not only the provision of secure units within community homes but also joint finance within the health system, the urban programme and the funding available under Section 11 of the Local Government Act 1966 for programmes related to ethnic minorities. **We recommend that consideration should be given to the establishment of an appropriate system of joint financing for the development of intermediate treatment.**

Attendance centres

80. Like the White Paper, we regard the attendance centre as "one of the most useful non-custodial penalties for young offenders". Most centres are open on Saturday afternoons, and the period of attendance ordered by the court (between 12 and 24 hours) is normally divided into sessions of two hours each. Half the session is taken up with physical education and the remainder with activities which may include craftwork and instruction in such topics as first aid, lifesaving, road safety and motor mechanics. Home Office Research Study No. 60, "Junior Attendance Centres" (1980), found that junior attendance centres

"appear to be satisfactorily achieving the objectives set them by the courts, that they are used for a wide variety of offenders and that there are no contra-indications to their continued use for any particular type of boy. Their use might, indeed, be extended to include some of those to whom the courts reluctantly award custodial penalties."

81. In 1979 attendance centre orders were imposed on 13 per cent of boys and 1 per cent of girls aged 14-16 convicted of indictable offences and offences triable either way. The percentages for those aged 10 and under 14 were 17 per cent and less than ½ per cent respectively.

82. Section 7 of the Children and Young Persons Act 1969 envisaged the phasing out of junior attendance centres; yet these provide a cheap, straight-forward penalty without the undesirable side effects of custody. The average cost of an attendance centre order in the financial year 1979-80 was about £35. In 1975 the Expenditure Committee recommended "that attendance centres be retained and that, where possible, the system be extended", and the present Government shares this view. At the beginning of 1979, there were 71 junior attendance centres for boys aged 10 and under 17. Since then the Government has expanded the system of junior centres to 101, including 6 for girls and 3 mixed centres for both boys and girls, and four more centres are planned. In its comments on the White Paper, the National Association of Probation Officers proposed that careful research should accompany the development of attendance centres "so that the stated aim to take an increasing proportion of those juvenile offenders currently sent into custody can be tested."

83. Until last year there were only two attendance centres for the 17-21 age group — a centre in Manchester established in 1958 and one established in Greenwich in 1964. In 1978 facilities in eight junior attendance centres in the West Midlands and West Yorkshire were extended to include offenders aged 17

and 18 for an experimental period of three years.

84. The White Paper, "The Reduction of Pressure on the Prison System", (1980) stated:

> "Courts which have had senior attendance centres available to them have found them useful, particularly to impose a temporary loss of leisure on immature young people as a suitable reminder that their criminal behaviour will not be tolerated. The two existing senior centres at Manchester and Greenwich are therefore no longer regarded as experimental and the Government intends to increase the number of such centres as quickly as possible" (para. 101).

85. The Government has asked five Chief Constables to open senior attendance centres in their areas. Two new senior centres were opened last year in Nottingham and Newcastle and further centres are planned to cater for the West Midlands, Leicester and Merseyside. In response to our recommendation in "Too Many Prisoners" that senior attendance centres should be established on a national basis, the Home Secretary has confirmed that the Government intends to establish such centres in at least the main centres of population, subject to review in the light of experience with the current expansion.

86. **We recommend that the provision of the Children and Young Persons Act 1969 for the phasing out of attendance centres should be repealed; that the number of junior and senior attendance centres should be increased until both types of centre are available to courts in at least all the main centres of population for offenders of both sexes; that links should be developed between attendance centres and intermediate treatment schemes, so that young offenders wishing to continue participation in constructive activities after the expiry of the attendance centre order can be channelled into voluntary participation in intermediate treatment; and that careful research should accompany the extension of attendance centres, to monitor the extent to which they are used for offenders who would otherwise receive custodial sentences.**

Fines and recognisances

87. The fine is the most commonly used of all the penalties available to the courts and, in terms of reconviction rates, appears to be slightly more effective than other forms of sentence for offenders with similar characteristics. In 1979, 54 per cent of males and 52 per cent of females aged 17 and 21 convicted of indictable or triable-either-way offences were fined. In our report "Too Many Prisoners" we endorsed the Expenditure Committee's view in its report "The Reduction of Pressure on the Prison System" (1978) that

> "One of the main ways of reducing the pressure on prisons would be to fine more offenders, especially young adult offenders who are in regular employment."

We recommend that there should be a greater use of the fine for young adult offenders.

88. 37 per cent of boys and 39 per cent of girls aged 14 and 17 convicted of indictable and triable-either-way offences in 1979 were fined. At present a court may (and if the offender is under 14 must) order the parents to pay a fine im-

posed on a juvenile, unless it is satisfied that the parents have not conduced to the commission of the offence by neglecting to exercise due care and control of the child or young person. The White Paper states that there has been no clear judicial interpretation of the scope of these provisions and claims that there is some evidence that the courts have been reluctant to use them because of uncertainty as to their ambit. It proposed to "strengthen and clarify" these provisions, so that parents will be required to pay fines imposed on children under 17 "unless, in the particular circumstances of the case, a court thinks it would be unreasonable to make them pay", and suggests that

> "this clarification and extension of the law will encourage the courts to assert the duty of parents to act responsibly towards their children and take all steps within their power to prevent them committing criminal offences" (para. 54).

89. The courts also have power, with the consent of the parent or guardian, to make an order requiring the parent or guardian to enter into a recognisance to take proper care of the juvenile and exercise proper control over him. The White Paper argues that this power "can also be a most effective way of securing the co-operation of parents in the prevention of delinquent behaviour" (para. 55). It therefore proposes to increase the amount of financial recognisance which parents can be ordered to forfeit if they fail to fulfil the undertaking they make to the court.

90. Some commentators have questioned whether the Government's proposals would either improve or clarify the present law. For example, the "New Law Journal" commented in an editorial of 16 October 1980 that

> ". . . so far from 'simplifying and clarifying' the existing provisions on which those powers depend, the substitution in the proposed redefinition of 'in the particular circumstances of the case a court thinks . . . ' for a proviso expressed in the comparatively clear and objective terms of 'failure to exercise due care and control' is likely only to have precisely the opposite effect and to give rise to serious inconsistencies and injustice in practice. Certainly, the White Paper makes no attempt to explain in what 'particular circumstances' other than failure to exercise due care and control, it will be appropriate for a court to make a parent liable for payment of a fine."

91. While there are some types of case in which it would be appropriate to oblige parents to pay fines imposed on juvenile offenders, there are other cases in which such a course could be both unreasonable and harmful. In some cases where a young offender is at odds with his parents, the resentment resulting from the imposition of a fine on the parents could damage family relationships even further, thereby placing the young person more at risk than ever. In some cases magistrates may consider that, if the fine is to have any value, this will lie in its being paid by the child himself rather than in his parents, relieving him of the financial responsibility for payment. In other cases, the parent may have done everything that could reasonably be expected to discipline and control the young person, and **we recommend that a fine should not be imposed on the**

parents of a juvenile offender unless there is clear evidence that parental responsibilities have been neglected.

92. The Conference of Chief Probation Officers points out in its comments on the White Paper that the power to require parents to pay fines imposed on their children under 17 will need to be exercised sensitively if it is to be productive and avoid the risk of exacerbating family problems. It suggests that social enquiry reports could comment more substantially than at present on the possibility of court decisions involving the responsibility of parents, including the power to require parents to enter into recognisances "which could usefully be developed to enlist co-operation in community-based measures."

93. **We recommend that legislation concerning the imposition of fines on the parents of juvenile offenders should specify factors which the courts should take into account in deciding whether this course would be unreasonable in the particular case.** These might include whether the parents have neglected to exercise due care and control of the child; whether it is desirable that the child himself should assume responsibility for payment; and the child's relationship with his parents and the likely effect on family relationships of requiring the parents to pay. **We further recommend that social enquiry reports should comment more substantially than at present on the implications of possible court decisions involving the responsibility of parents.**

Community service for young offenders

94. We are convinced of the central role which forms of community service have to play in the development of community-based provision for young offenders. While some forms of community service for offenders contain a punitive element in the compulsory deprivation of leisure time, community service also enables offenders to take advantage of opportunities for constructive achievement, to appreciate the needs of disadvantaged and handicapped members of the community and to make reparation to the community against which they have offended. Above all, community service emphasises the development of the offender's positive qualities rather than merely the punishment or containment of his negative ones.

a) Community service orders

95. Community service orders, first introduced in 1973 in six experimental areas, are now available to courts throughout England and Wales for offenders aged 17 and over. The offender is required to work unpaid for a specified number of hours which must be completed within twelve months, and the Home Office Research Unit has estimated that 45 to 50 per cent of those given community service orders receive them as an alternative to imprisonment. Of the community service orders terminated in 1979, 74 per cent were recorded as being completed satisfactorily. It is essential in our view that community service orders should be strictly enforced and not seen as a soft option.

96. About half the community service orders made relate to people aged 17 and under 21 and, as the White Paper comments, the community service order "has clearly provided the courts with a very effective alternative to custodial sentences, particularly with young adult offenders". In 1979 7,989 community service orders were imposed on young adult offenders: 7 per cent of young adult

males and 2 per cent of young adult females convicted of indictable or triable-either-way offences received community service orders during that year. In its evidence to us, the Commission for Racial Equality suggested that young black people receive a disproportionately high number of custodial sentences in comparison with their white counterparts and advocated the use of ethnic minority organisations as locations where community service orders might be carried out.

97. The White Paper proposes that the community service order should be available for 16 year olds who have committed imprisonable offences. This proposal is opposed by the British Association of Social Workers, the National Association of Probation Officers and the National Youth Bureau, but was supported by the Association of Directors of Social Services, the Association of Metropolitan Authorities and the Conference of Chief Probation Officers in their comments on the White Paper; by the Howard League for Penal Reform in its comments on the last Government's Green Paper, "Youth Custody and Supervision: A new Sentence"*; and by the Justices' Clerks' Society in its recent paper on child law reform. The Conference of Chief Probation Officers suggests that for 16 year olds receiving full time education the maximum number of hours of community service should be 120; that there should be an intensified ratio of supervisory staff to workers; and that community service for 16 year olds should be developed in a small number of areas in the first instance.

98. Two principal arguments are put forward by those members of the probation and after-care service who are concerned about the extension of community service orders to 16 year olds, and by NACRO which has also expressed reservations about the proposal. First, it is argued that 17 year olds are currently regarded by community service organisers as their most difficult age group and that 16 year olds may be even more unreliable. Secondly, it is suggested that the extension of community service orders to 16 year olds may devalue the sentence and lead to its being regarded as a comparatively light penalty rather than principally as an alternative to custody. However, on both these points the remedy lies squarely in the hands of the probation service, since courts make community service orders in the light of recommendations from the probation service about offenders' suitability for community service. As with adult offenders, careful selection must therefore be exercised to ensure that the 16 year olds who receive community service orders are suitable for this disposition and that orders are used as an alternative to custody. The development of any non-custodial option is accompanied by the danger that it will be used as an alternative to other non-custodial sentences. This is a weak and insufficient argument against the provision of non-custodial options which are desirable in themselves, and is rather an argument for circular guidance or statutory guidelines which would encourage their use for offenders of all ages who would otherwise have received custodial sentences.

99. **We recommend that there should be a continuing extension of community service orders. We further recommend that community service orders should be available for 16 year olds, and the probation service should receive adequate**

---

* Hereafter, all allusions in this report to "the Green Paper" refer to the Green Paper "Youth Custody and Supervision: A New Sentence" (1978).

additional resources in recognition of the careful selection and close supervision required for this age group.

b)   Community service within intermediate treatment

100. The Association of Directors of Social Services observed in its comments on the White Paper that

> "particularly for juveniles, community service could be improved if, for some offenders, it could be linked to some form of supervision. This could be achieved by including community service as a condition of an intermediate treatment supervision order, as well as an order in its own right".

101. A number of intermediate treatment schemes involve young people in forms of community service. Typically, these constitute one element in a diverse programme of activities. Examples of community service undertaken by those taking part in intermediate treatment programmes of which we are aware include visiting elderly people and shopping, gardening and decorating for them, visiting hospitals, distributing fostering leaflets, helping with summer playschemes and in a youth club for the mentally handicapped, extending an adventure playground and fund-raising activities.

102. Of particular interest is the Norwich Community Work Project, which began in 1979, whereby the courts use supervision orders with an I.T. condition in order to impose what is effectively a community service order on youngsters aged between 14 and 17 at risk of a custodial sentence. The condition is made for a fixed number of hours to be carried out within six months. The young offenders are involved in one of three schemes:

a)   Converting a garage into a workshop and constructing playground equipment for the under fives.

b)   Conversion of another garage into a store for camping equipment and making equipment for a playgroup.

c)   Working as a junior youth leader, organising and supervising under twelves at a YMCA junior youth club.

103. If the stipulated hours are successfully completed, the young person may be returned to court with a recommendation for discharge of the supervision order. Failure to complete the hours brings the young person back to court, and the court can impose the usual sanctions for failure to comply with a supervision order – normally a fine or an attendance centre order. (In a few cases the court defers sentence for six months instead of making a supervision order).

104. So far 18 participants have been through the scheme, each of whom had an average of over 20 previous offences and several of whom had previously experienced detention centre or care orders. To date only two have re-offended. The project costs £150 per child per year. A similar scheme is in operation in Bradford.

105. **We recommend that forms of community service for juvenile offenders should be developed within intermediate treatment programmes and should be used in particular as an alternative to custodial and residential disposals.**

c)   *The New Careers Project*

106. The National Association of Probation Officers has drawn our attention to the New Careers Project, established in 1973 by the Bristol Association for the Care and Resettlement of Offenders. This scheme takes young adult offenders committed to the Crown Court for sentence and likely to receive custodial sentences. As an alternative to custody, they receive a two year probation order, with a one year condition of residence at the project.

107. The project provides training based on practical work projects within social services settings including psychiatric and subnormality hospitals, intermediate treatment projects, day centres, a primary school, a school for ESN children, playgroups, old people's homes, hostels, advice centres and homes for the handicapped. New students undertake a series of observation placements for a week at a time, together with one-off activities such as removal or painting jobs for the social services department. For the next six months they work three days a week on a series of placements, each lasting for six weeks, combined with training in social skills and training related to the student's practical work. Thereafter, the student opts for a final full time placement which is designed to lead directly or indirectly to employment: this may or may not be in the social work field depending on the student's preference. Most students have permanent jobs arranged before leaving the project, and many of these are in social services settings.

108. The National Association of Probation Officers comments:

> "The experience of the New Careers Project has shown that it is possible for highly delinquent young offenders to engage in demanding social work tasks and successfully redirect their energies in a valuable and constructive manner. At present the programme is operated within the context of a hostel but it could be adapted to function in a community setting as well, developing the unique experience of ex-offenders in a way which would allow them to contribute to the well-being of others."

109. **We recommend that schemes involving selected young adult offenders in full time training based on work in social services settings, in combination with a probation order and with a view to obtaining full time employment in due course, should be more widely developed.**

d)   *The Child in Care Scheme*

110. The potential of community service for juvenile offenders is illustrated by "Give and Take" (1980), the Dartington Social Research Unit's research report into the first three years of the Child in Care Scheme, a project initiated by Community Service Volunteers which provides full time community service placements for young people aged 15-18 in the care of social services departments in Bolton, East Sussex, Haringey, Lambeth, Suffolk and Wandsworth. The DHSS funded the scheme's administrative costs and the salaries of the project organisers, while the local authorities provided the volunteers' pocket money and a small travel and subsistence allowance, and office accommodation for the project organisers.

111. During the scheme's first three years, 432 young people were referred by social workers for placement. 59 per cent were offenders and 27 per cent had

been convicted on more than six occasions. 18 per cent had committed an offence involving violence. For most of the young people, the alternative to participation in the scheme would have been either to remain in or to enter residential care, and about 20 per cent would have gone to detention centres or borstals. An examination of the most recent referrals to the scheme indicates a growing number whose offences are continuous and serious and who are clear candidates for CHEs and penal establishments.

112. The young people are paid a basic rate of £7.50 per week together with such expenses as travelling and lunch costs. However, for the older volunteers the local authorities increase these payments so that they do not fall below social security benefits. The most common forms of work are with the physically and mentally handicapped, with the aged and with pre-school children in nurseries and playgroups. Many are also involved in community work, such as community centres, advice centres, law centres and citizens' rights centres. Others are assisting home helps and working in occupational therapy.

113. In 55 per cent of cases, the young people's supervisors stated that they worked very well. 30 per cent said that their performance was satisfactory and in only 6 per cent was the volunteer's contribution classified as poor. 67 per cent of the volunteers had obtained permanent jobs within two months of leaving the scheme. The research report states:

> "The scheme seems to achieve what has eluded so many other reformatory approaches — a significant fall in offending among persistent adolescent delinquents."

114. A survey was undertaken of all volunteers, nine months after they had completed their last placements. 21 per cent had been convicted of an offence, mostly petty thefts for which they were fined or conditionally discharged. A number of the participants appeared before the courts while on the scheme (several of whom were awaiting court appearances when they joined) and

> "Generally, magistrates looked approvingly on the projects and frequently the social workers and organisers asked that the offender be allowed to continue participation. Magistrates usually accepted this recommendation as it offered a reasonable and controlling alternative to placing the young person in a secure remand."

All the original schemes have now been taken over by the local authorities themselves and new schemes have been set up in Birmingham, Sunderland and Devon and Cornwall.

115. **We recommend that schemes providing community service placements for difficult and delinquent young people in care should be further developed.**

e)   Restitution schemes
116. Mr John Harding, Deputy Chief Probation Officer for the West Midlands, has provided the working party with a report on restitution programmes for both juveniles and adults in the U.S.A., based on a visit he made in May 1980 to six states — Massachusetts, Maine, Minnesota, California, Louisiana and Mississipi. Such schemes take various forms. Some involve the offender in locating a job and making monetary compensation to the victim or to community organisa-

tions. In others, local firms provide a certain number of hours paid work at minimum wage rates from which the restitution payments are made. In some schemes offenders perform forms of community service for which they are paid an allowance which is used to pay back their victims.

117. Some restitution programmes for adult offenders are residential, taking participants who have served a period of imprisonment into a community-based hostel, where they obtain jobs with the help of the staff and repay an agreed amount of money from their earnings to the victim. In addition, they are normally expected to perform some unpaid community service at the weekends. Normally the offender makes contributions towards the cost of his upkeep at the hostel, the upkeep of his family and court costs, and compensates the victim with agreed restitution payments. In some cases, offenders who have committed victimless crimes pay an indirect form of restitution to a fund for the compensation of certain categories of victims.

118. We have found particularly interesting those schemes which draw up restitution contracts with the participation of the offender, the victim and a mediator, whereby the amount and nature of compensation is agreed. Sometimes community service is performed in addition to cash restitution. A form of restitution used in a small number of cases is victim service, which involves the offender working for the victim, either to repair the actual damage done or to provide service equal to the amount of financial loss caused by the offence.

119. Restitution schemes involving such mediation have several attractions. First, they confront the offender directly with the suffering which his behaviour has caused to the victim. Secondly, the victim is involved in the process in a positive manner and not merely used as aid to the prosecution in proving the offender's guilt. Thirdly, such schemes involve the offender in making restitution either directly to the victim or to the wider community in a manner approved by and agreed with the victim.

120. We note that the report of the Dunpark Committee on Reparation by the Offender to the Victim in Scotland (1977) recommended that reporters should be directed to bear in mind the possibility of children performing some act or services for the benefit of their victims as an alternative to prosecution and that children's hearings should be instructed to have regard to reparation as a possible treatment measure for child offenders. It also recommended that greater consideration should be given by hearings to the possibility and practicability of inserting reparation conditions in supervision orders.

121. **We recommend that restitution schemes for young offenders should be established on an experimental basis in a few areas.** In the case of juvenile offenders, these could form a part of intermediate treatment provision, while for young adults they could be used in combination with a probation order. **These experiments should be carefully monitored and the results used as a basis for assessing whether this approach should be developed more widely.**

Probation "packages" and related schemes for young adults
122. There has been a sharp decline in the percentage of people aged 17 and under 21 convicted of indictable or triable-either-way offences who receive pro-

bation orders — from 14 per cent in 1969 to 7 per cent in 1979 for males and from 32 per cent to 19 per cent in the case of females. One approach which aims to halt and reverse this decline is described by the National Association of Probation Officers in its evidence to us:

"There is a growing trend in the presentation of a 'probation package' to the courts in the form of a clearly stated programme of various activities and methods of intervention which is spelt out in the Social Enquiry Report (e.g. a typical 'package' might be involvement in a day centre, coupled with participation in a social skills course). This way of presenting probation as a viable alternative demonstrates to the court that specific concrete intervention is going to take place under the terms of the order."

123. The potential scope for using probation "packages" as an alternative to custody is illustrated by a recent survey, "Sending Young Adults Down" by Philippa Merriman (1981), published by the University of Lancaster's Centre of Youth, Crime and Community, which analysed the cases of 100 young adults sentenced to custody in Lancaster and Morecambe. The majority had been convicted of offences against property, most of which had involved damage or loss of less than £100. Panels of probation officers who assessed in how many cases alternatives to custody might have been possible considered that in 15 cases immediate custody was inevitable and in a further four cases custody could be suspended. They recommended that probation orders combined with a hostel place or other supported accommodation would have been appropriate for 19 offenders; probation orders with a day centre condition for 13 offenders; and probation orders combined with both a day centre and supported accommodation for five offenders. (In a further 19 cases, a probation order or intensive supervision without a "package" element was considered appropriate).

124. This approach depends for its credibility on the availability of a range of residential and non-residential facilities which can be presented to the courts in combination with a probation recommendation as viable alternatives to custody. Our recommendation in "Too Many Prisoners" that there should be a greatly increased provision of housing and hostels, day centres and employment schemes for offenders is therefore of particular importance in this connection.

125. Many young adult offenders have accommodation problems, and homelessness and instability often contribute towards their criminal behaviour. In "Young Adult Offenders" (1974), the Advisory Council on the Penal System stated that there was a

"great need for further hostels and other supportive accommodation for young offenders, both for those who are released from custody and those who, given the right kind of residential support, do not need to be removed from the community at all" (para. 412).

126. The Conference of Chief Probation Officers commented in its observations on the Green Paper that many young offenders are either homeless or living in situations of such conflict at home that they commit "survival" offences or offences which have their roots in aimless drifting. The Conference argued that a variety of accommodation is needed offering a range of facilities "from the in-

formality of bed sitters, through landladies schemes to hostel provision". A recent survey of relevant research by NACRO's senior research officer concluded that homelessness is an important factor in reconviction, and that for the younger age groups at least the chances of reconviction for homeless young offenders are twice as high as for those with a home.

127. The White Paper "The Reduction of Pressure on the Prison System" (June 1980) stated that the Home Office currently grant aids over 200 voluntary hostels providing over 2,400* places for ex-offenders and added that "it is hoped that resources will be found to extend this provision in the future". However, the number of hostel places for the young adult age group is very limited and hostel accommodation is unpopular with many of this age group: surveys which have examined young people's accommodation preferences show that one of their major requirements is independence.

128. Single young adults who have left home, or who have no parental home, have traditionally looked to the private rented sector for accommodation. This has become increasingly difficult to obtain, both because two million units of accommodation have been lost over the last twenty years in this sector, and because there has been an explosion of demand for housing suitable for small households as a result of increasing demands by young people for independent accommodation and of increases in the rate of divorce and separation and in the number of old people. Many private landlords are wary of housing young people, especially those in receipt of supplementary benefit, and often require large deposits which young people with low earnings or on supplementary benefit cannot afford. Single people have no general right to public housing in the way that those with children do. Although housing authorities have an obligation to provide housing to certain groups of homeless people, including vulnerable single people, in practice this obligation is interpreted in a very limited way. While housing associations provide small units and are concerned about special need groups, their provision is now in great demand and young adults do not necessarily have high priority. All these problems affect young homeless people generally: a criminal record often further diminishes a young adult's chance of finding suitable accommodation.

129. NACRO argued in its comments on the Green Paper that the range of accommodation facilities needed includes emergency short stay facilities to provide immediate shelter and help for residents in working out where they should go next; hostel accommodation providing communal living with the support of full time residential staff; self-catering accommodation units providing more independence but with certain communal facilities and with support from non-residential staff; independent accommodation such as flats and houses, without regular support or supervision but with support from a social worker available if necessary; and general housing provision, in particular fair rent housing provided by housing associations or local authority tenancies for single people.

130. In many cases, participation by a young offender in an employment scheme can appropriately constitute part of a "package". Recent research by

---

*   The number is now nearly 2,700

Steven Box and Chris Hale of the University of Kent has found that every increase of 1,000 unemployed young people results in an additional increase of 56 young people sentenced to custody over and above the increase commensurate with the crime rate. The recent NACRO report "Services to Unemployed Offenders" (1980) stated that "the courts place considerable importance on the question of employment when sentencing decisions are being made" and pointed out that courts will often defer sentence to give the offender the opportunity either to find work or to establish a satisfactory job record. It suggested that in many cases courts have imposed non-custodial sentences on the strength of the offender's employment prospects or, more recently, offers of places on YOP and STEP schemes.

131 YOP (the Youth Opportunities Programme) provides training and work experience for unemployed young people up to the age of 19. STEP (the Special Temporary Employment Programme) provided temporary work for adults who had been out of work for six months in the case of 19-24 year olds and twelve months for those who are older. (From 1981-82 STEP has been replaced by the Community Enterprise Programme which caters for those of 18 and over, and both programmes are being considerably expanded. CEP programmes, which involve higher remuneration than YOP schemes, may be particularly attractive to many young adults, especially those who are living in accommodation away from their families or who are financially independent of them).

132. The Probation and After-care Service and a number of voluntary organisations have taken advantage of Manpower Services Commission finance to establish YOP and CEP schemes for unemployed ex-offenders. Since 1978 the Home Office has financed NACRO's Employment Development Unit, which develops projects for unemployed offenders financed by the Manpower Services Commission. The Unit has established 17 YOP projects providing 644 places for young offenders and a further 138 YOP places have been established in projects for offenders sponsored by other bodies. NACRO's existing YOP schemes are to expand by 160 places to 800 in total in the near future and the Association hopes to establish a further twelve schemes with 430 places for young offenders.

133. The importance of such schemes, of the workshop schemes for offenders managed by such agencies as NACRO and the Burnbake Trust and of the Apex Trust's employment preparation schemes for young offenders is even greater now than when the Manpower Services Commission's special programmes began. A working party on the employment of offenders established in 1979 by the Conference of Chief Probation Officers found that the proportion of those with whom probation officers are dealing who were then unemployed varied from 25 per cent to 70 per cent. A recent survey by the Apex Trust suggests that the situation has deteriorated rapidly since then, and NACRO's YOP schemes report that the demand for places is in most instances more than double what it was a year ago. A person on a probation officer's case load is between three and five times more likely to be out of work than a non-offender from the same area; yet, as Mr. Leon Brittan Q.C., M.P., commented in a speech to the Apex Trust on 12 December 1980, "few would dispute that an offender on a supported work scheme or in full time employment is less likely to be tempted to re-offend than one who is not occupied".

134. In some areas attendance at a day centre provides an additional option which can be incorporated in a probation "package". The facilities and aims of day centres vary, but include provision of a meeting place and a range of activities for socially isolated offenders; information, advice and counselling; social skills training; literacy training and other educational opportunities; and in some cases specialised help for such groups as drug users and problem drinkers.

135. Several day centre projects which are primarily concerned with the education of offenders are increasingly being used by the courts as an alternative to a short prison sentence. Although open to the whole age range, many such projects find themselves dealing with a high proportion of young adults. One example is the Swindon Basic Education Unit, established in 1977 by the Wiltshire Probation Service and NACRO, which has been run by the Probation Service since April 1980. The centre opens each weekday morning and, using a combination of group work and one-to-one tuition with volunteer tutors, enables offenders to acquire literacy, numeracy and skills in communication, language and study. At any one time some twenty students are regularly attending the centre and, during its second year of operation, 70 students had contact with the project. The average length of stay is about three months and most of the students leave to take up full time education or to go on to TOPS and other courses. Few of those leaving the unit have re-offended.

136. Some 50 day centres are now known to the Home Office as having been set up by the probation service or by voluntary bodies with the aid of a Home Office grant. However, as a recent report by the Howard League for Penal Reform, "A Chance to Change" by Elizabeth Burney (1980), pointed out:

"The geographical spread of those centres is very uneven. Apart from a few keen areas like Surrey and Hampshire, London and the South-East are badly served compared with, for example, the North-West. The North as a whole has relatively more to offer than the South or Midlands, the Western shire counties much more than, say, East Anglia".

137. The White Paper "The Reduction of Pressure on the Prison System" (1980) accepted the Expenditure Committee's recommendation in 1978 that more day centres should be provided and said that both the statutory services and voluntary organisations would be given further encouragement to undertake the task. It added, however, that this would "require additional resources which will necessarily limit the rate of progress" (para. 99).

138. In some instances, assistance with problems concerning dependence on drugs or alcohol can form part of a probation "package". In England and Wales there are at present 78 alcohol treatment units within the National Health Service, 72 residential establishments and three day centres for problem drinkers, with a wide variety of approaches to the rehabilitation of those with severe drink problems. Several of these schemes have reported that the average age of those coming forward for assistance is falling.

139. In our earlier report "Too Many Prisoners" we recommended that a range of residential and non-residential facilities should be provided for drug dependents. There are currently 267 places in rehabilitative hostels for drug users managed by voluntary organisations and seven non-residential "street" agencies

working in five cities for people with drug problems. Many areas, however, have no formal treatment facilities and virtually no services with expertise in handling drug related problems.

140. Over the past few years there has been an increase in the number of drug addicts known to the Home Office and the street level agencies have also had an increased number of clients who are not notified. At the same time increasing financial pressure has resulted in a gradual restriction of services. In consequence, "as supplies of illicit opiates destined for the UK market have increased, and problem drug use has escalated, there has been a reduction in the facilities available to assist drug dependents" (Annual Report for 1979-80, Standing Conference on Drug Abuse).

141. In real terms, grant aid received by the street level agencies from statutory sources has declined in value in the recent past. The need for major economies has obliged nearly all these agencies to reduce their staffing or to leave posts vacant, and a loss of one member of staff can mean a 25 per cent reduction. In at least two instances, organisations have reduced their staffing by 50 per cent. We are pleased to note that several organisations have received exceptional grants from the DHSS to cover their deficit in the financial year 1980-81, allowing them to bring their staffing levels up to full establishment again; but these grants have only temporarily deferred the need to reduce services.

142. Of the 267 beds in rehabilitation houses in the United Kingdom, only 39 have been added since 1973, an increase of 17.2 per cent during a period in which first notifications to the Home Office have increased by 100 per cent. Three out of every four applications for admission to a rehabilitation house are unsuccessful, and the realisation that there is a long waiting list often deters drug users from seeking rehabilitation. There has been a gradual shift in recent years from "block" funding to funding of individual cases on a per capita basis by the Supplementary Benefits Commission, local probation committees and social services departments. The Standing Conference on Drug Abuse points out that administering a system of funding where fees are paid by an authority for an individual resident is costly and time-consuming. Different authorities operate a variety of application procedures, and there are considerable delays between the date of submission of the application and agreement by the authority to fund. At best, this can cause severe cash flow problems; at worst the resident is accommodated for several months at a loss to the rehabilitation house, and funding is then refused. Many authorities have refused to accept new applications for funding, having previously accepted responsibility for the fees of an individual, because of reductions in their budgets.

143. We strongly endorse the view of the Standing Conference, which was expressed as follows in its annual report for 1979-80:

"As social and health services become less able to cope, penal resources will become the major response to drug misuse. This does not represent any saving in public expenditure, merely the transfer of resources from a potentially effective to a palpably ineffective method of dealing with the problem. The voluntary organisations, which provide all the street level and rehabilitation services in the country, offer the only positive intervention. It is essential that their work is adequately supported."

144. **We recommend that the Home Secretary should issue guidance encouraging the further development of probation "packages", whereby a clearly stated programme of activities and methods of intervention is spelled out to the court in a social enquiry report.** We further recommend that there should be a greatly increased provision for those under 21 of hostels and other forms of accommodation, day centres, educational and employment schemes and facilities for drug dependents and problem drinkers. Where there are conflicting demands on resources, priority should be given to facilities for this age group.

145. National funding is available for hostels and other forms of accommodation from the Home Office and the Department of the Environment, for employment schemes from the Manpower Services Commission and for day centres from the Home Office. In the case of facilities for drug dependents and problem drinkers, however, no permanent system of central government funding exists and the financial viability of schemes is dependent on the varying priorities of local authorities and health authorities. The paucity of such facilities in relation to the need makes the establishment of schemes for problem drinkers and drug misusers, and the survival of existing schemes, a matter of more than merely local significance. Moreover, since after-care hostels for offenders managed by voluntary organisations are eligible for permanent funding from the Home Office, it seems illogical that rehabilitative hostels for ex-offenders with alcohol or drug problems are not eligible for a similar permanent system of central government funding. **We recommend that a permanent system of central government funding for facilities for problem drinkers and drug misusers should be established.**

146. In our report "Too Many Prisoners" we recommended that each probation area should ensure that information is collated about accommodation, employment and day centre provision in its area and that all probation officers preparing social enquiry reports are provided with full and up to date information about facilities which could potentially be used as an alternative to imprisonment. **We recommend that each probation area should identify the gaps in provision for young adult offenders and, in co-operation with social services departments and other relevant agencies, should develop a strategy to fill those gaps.**

Co-operation between agencies working with juveniles
147. In its report of 1975, the Expenditure Committee recommended that liaison committees representing magistrates, teachers, social workers and probation officers, and with police officers attending where appropriate, should be set up in every local authority "to discuss not only the progress of individual children in care or under supervision, but also more general matters such as the development of intermediate treatment."

148. The White Paper referred favourably to the Expenditure Committee's emphasis on the importance of communication and co-operation between all the agencies concerned with juveniles and said:

"The Government cannot emphasise too strongly the importance it attaches to such local co-operation."

149. As a result of a circular issued jointly by the Home Office, the Department of Health and Social Security, the Department of Education and Science and the Welsh Office in December 1978, chief officers of police reported on the arrangements in their areas for consultation and co-operation between the agencies concerned with juvenile delinquency. A further circular was issued in August 1980 giving a general account of these developments. The White Paper commented that this showed that

"where local co-operation is good, a much more effective response to the problems of juveniles and a better use of resources can be achieved by avoiding unnecessary and confusing duplication of effort" (para. 36).

In its evidence to us, the National Association of Probation Officers also emphasised the importance of joint planning between agencies.

150. We regard co-operation between agencies dealing with young offenders as essential to the development of a coherent policy to reduce crime among young people. **We recommend that in all local authority areas arrangements should be made for regular consultation between those agencies which are concerned with young offenders and young people at risk.**

151. It is clear from the report of the joint working party of the Magistrates' Association and the local authority associations on the Children and Young Persons Act 1969 (July 1978) that arrangements for local consultation, though widespread, are patchy in their development. It pointed out that arrangements which depend on personal contacts are frequently jeopardised by staff turnover; that few areas have established formal consultative machinery; and that no formal or regular meetings are held at regional level, although some regions have organised conferences and seminars, for example on intermediate treatment, and most regional planning committees have co-opted magistrates and representatives of other organisations. There may be one liaison committee for an area, or several committees. Sometimes all the bodies concerned with juvenile offenders and children at risk are represented, while sometimes representation is only of a few bodies and some interests are completely omitted. There are considerable variations in the frequency of meetings of formal committees and, where the arrangements are informal, contacts appear to be generally less frequent.

152. This report rightly argued that "the main purpose of consultation is not decision-making as such and the responsible bodies will and should retain the final word" and it set out a number of guidelines for local consultation. Despite its acknowledgment of the patchy and variable nature of consultative machinery, it considered that it would be wrong to prescribe any single pattern of consultation and argued:

"Different parts of the country have different needs and priorities. There are dangers associated with imposing a uniform pattern; it would be pointless to disrupt existing arrangements which have proved satisfactory; and it would be undesirable to stifle initiatives, by forcing adherence to a national plan."

It recommended therefore that there should be no attempt to impose or to encourage the development of a uniform system of consultation and that local areas should be able to establish the kind of arrangements that seem suitable for their requirements both as to the form of the meetings and as to their frequency.

153. The report also proposed that there could usefully be more consultation at regional planning level through the children's regional planning committees, and that this could most usefully be achieved by juvenile court magistrates being represented. It therefore recommended that those regional planning committees which had not yet done so should consider co-opting magistrates who would contribute to their work. To date nine of the twelve regional planning committees have co-opted magistrates. **We recommend that those children's regional planning committees which have not done so should co-opt magistrates.**

154. In its comments on the White Paper, New Approaches to Juvenile Crime expressed concern at "the patchy and variable nature of consultation and co-ordination in this area" and suggested that "it is perfectly possible for legislation to lay down minimum standards for consultation without stifling local initiative or enforcing a uniform pattern of consultation". It therefore proposed that local authorities should be required to establish inter-agency committees which would monitor patterns of juvenile crime and provision for juvenile offenders in the area, discuss and co-ordinate policies concerning juvenile delinquency and promote the establishment of a range of community-based schemes to deal with young offenders.

155. The White Paper, on the other hand, did not take the view that inter-agency co-operation could best be achieved by legislation:

> "Circumstances vary greatly from area to area and statutory requirements for the formation of specific consultative machinery may do as much to harm existing satisfactory local arrangements as to encourage consultation where none exists. The Government therefore intends to continue to do everything possible to encourage inter-agency co-operation at a local level without imposing any centralised formula" (para. 37).

156. **We recommend that there should be a thorough evaluation and monitoring of systems of co-ordination in several areas of the country with a view to producing guidelines for good practice which would be of national application. In the light of the results of this evaluation, the Government should consider whether a statutory duty should be imposed on local authorities to establish inter-agency committees to discuss and co-ordinate policies concerning juvenile delinquency.**

157. Home Office Circular 83/80 to Chief Officers of Police, "Juveniles: Co-operation Between the Police and Other Agencies", pointed out that, although there may be good working relationships between the various agencies in most areas, only a minority of agencies have regular arrangements for the inter-change of staff. Devon and Cornwall Constabulary are pioneering an attachment scheme whereby probation officers and social workers are attached to the police for one or two weeks, with reciprocal arrangements for constables and sergeants to be attached to probation and social services departments. Arrangements also exist for probation and police officers in Nottinghamshire and West Yorkshire to

change places for short periods. The circular commented:

> "It is clear that, where manpower restraints permit secondments, much can be done to increase the knowledge and understanding of other agencies' work by short periods of interchange."

158. **We recommend that arrangements for the inter-change of staff between agencies concerned with young offenders and young people at risk should be encouraged and developed more widely.**

Specialisation in work with juveniles

159. In its report of 1975, the Expenditure Committee referred to a widespread complaint that social workers with a general training lack the specialist knowledge and the opportunity to acquire the specialist experience necessary for the treatment of difficult juveniles. Noting that in some local authorities specialist posts were being created in such areas as intermediate treatment, fostering and court work, it commented:

> "We do not believe that acceptance of the principles of the Seebohm report made it necessary to abandon specialisation within the local authority social services departments, and are glad to see that some authorities are already moving away from the idea of having completely general social workers" (para. 97).

It recommended that some social workers should be encouraged to specialise in the field of juvenile delinquency. Referring to complaints about the lack of knowledge of court procedure shown by social workers appearing in court, the Committee also recommended that "attention be given to ensuring that social workers are trained in court procedure."

160. The British Association of Social Workers, in its report of 1978 on the Children and Young Persons Act 1969, proposed that specialists should be appointed for work with juvenile offenders and that social workers should receive sufficient training in basic legal procedures and the giving of evidence to enable them to function with confidence in the juvenile court. Observing that few basic professional courses adequately cover this area, it proposed that local authorities should therefore undertake in-service training to meet this need.

161. New Approaches to Juvenile Crime in its memorandum of March 1980 also argued for an increasing degree of specialisation in work with juveniles "which would constitute a logical development of the establishment of specialist local authority posts in such areas as intermediate treatment and court work." **We recommend that more social workers should be encouraged to specialise in work with juveniles and those working with this age group should receive appropriate specialised training, including training in court procedure.**

Summary of recommendations

1. Professional fostering schemes should be supported and extended and the DHSS should give local authorities positive guidance and encouragement to develop such schemes (para. 51).

2. There should be a range of intermediate treatment, catering both for young offenders and those at risk. Within this range, greater efforts should be made to provide intermediate treatment for juveniles who would otherwise have been committed to custodial and residential establishments (para. 61).

3. Before imposing an intermediate treatment requirement, the court should satisfy itself that the programme envisaged by the social worker or probation officer is appropriate (para. 67).

4. Intermediate treatment requirements should be mandatory and their implementation should not be left to the supervisor's discretion. However, discretion should be given to the supervising officer to modify the detailed content of the intermediate treatment programme in the light of changing circumstances (para. 67).

5. Local authorities should be encouraged to transfer resources from residential care to intermediate treatment. This transfer should be achieved in a manner which ensures that the resulting smaller scale residential sector is adequately financed with a complement of well trained and highly valued staff (para. 68).

6. The extra finance intended for the development of intermediate treatment which is to be added to the rate support grant should be increased to a level at least comparable with the extra £5 million necessitated by the proposed residential care order. This should be combined with a statutory requirement on local authorities to provide certain minimum levels of intermediate treatment (para. 69).

7. The probation service should be enabled to provide intermediate treatment facilities in a way which is consistent with proper co-ordination of local arrangements (para. 73).

8. There should be increased central government funding for intermediate treatment schemes run by voluntary organisations, and in particular there should be a considerable further increase in the funds available to the Rainer Foundation Intermediate Treatment Fund (para. 77).

9. Greater encouragement and support for voluntary initiatives in intermediate treatment should be provided by the statutory services (para. 77).

10. Consideration should be given to the establishment of an appropriate system of joint financing for the development of intermediate treatment (para. 79).

11. The provision of the Children and Young Persons Act 1969 for the phasing out of attendance centres should be repealed. The number of junior and senior attendance centres should be increased until both types of centre are available to courts in at least all the main centres of population for offenders of both sexes (para. 86).

12. Links should be developed between attendance centres and intermediate treatment schemes, so that young offenders wishing to continue participation in constructive activities after the expiry of the attendance order can

be channelled into voluntary participation in intermediate treatment (para. 86).

13. Careful research should accompany the extension of attendance centres, to monitor the extent to which they are used for offenders who would otherwise receive custodial sentences (para. 86).

14. There should be a greater use of the fine for young adult offenders (para. 87).

15. A fine should not be imposed on the parents of a juvenile offender unless there is clear evidence that parental responsibilities have been neglected (para. 91).

16. Legislation concerning the imposition of fines on the parents of juvenile offenders should specify factors which the courts should take into account in deciding whether this course would be unreasonable in the particular case (para. 93).

17. Social enquiry reports should comment more substantially than at present on the implications of possible court decisions involving the responsibility of parents (para. 93).

18. There should be a continuing extension of community service orders (para. 99).

19. Community service orders should be available for 16 year olds, and the probation service should receive adequate additional resources in recognition of the careful selection and close supervision required for this age group (para. 99).

20. Forms of community service for juvenile offenders should be developed within intermediate treatment programmes and should be used in particular as an alternative to custodial and residential disposals (para. 105).

21. Schemes involving selected young adult offenders in full time training based on work in social services settings, in combination with a probation order and with a view to obtaining full time employment in due course, should be more widely developed (para. 109).

22. Schemes providing community service placements for difficult and delinquent young people in care should be further developed (para. 115).

23. Restitution schemes for young offenders should be established on an experimental basis in a few areas. These experiments should be carefully monitored and the results used as a basis for assessing whether this approach should be developed more widely (para. 121).

24. The Home Secretary should issue guidance encouraging the further development of probation "packages", whereby a clearly stated programme of activities and methods of intervention is spelled out to the court in a social enquiry report (para. 144).

25. There should be a greatly increased provision for those under 21 of hostels and other forms of accommodation, day centres, educational and employment schemes, and facilities for drug dependents and problem drinkers.

Where there are conflicting demands on resources, priority should be given to facilities for this age group (para. 144).

26. A permanent system of central government funding for facilities for problem drinkers and drug misusers should be established (para. 145).

27. Each probation area should identify the gaps in provision for young adult offenders and, in co-operation with social services departments and other relevant agencies, should develop a strategy to fill those gaps (para. 146).

28. In all local authority areas arrangements should be made for regular consultation between those agencies which are concerned with young offenders and young people at risk (para. 150).

29. Those children's regional planning committees which have not yet done so should co-opt magistrates (para. 153).

30. There should be a thorough evaluation and monitoring of systems of co-ordination in several areas of the country with a view to producing guidelines for good practice which would be of national application. In the light of the results of this evaluation, the Government should consider whether a statutory duty should be imposed on local authorities to establish inter-agency committees to discuss and co-ordinate policies concerning juvenile delinquency (para. 156).

31. Arrangements for the inter-change of staff between agencies concerned with young offenders and young people at risk should be encouraged and developed more widely (para. 158).

32. More social workers should be encouraged to specialise in work with juveniles and those working with this age group should receive appropriate specialised training, including training in court procedure (para. 161).

IV: CARE ORDERS AND THE USE OF RESIDENTIAL CARE FOR YOUNG OFFENDERS

Care Orders

162. Care orders are available both in care proceedings and criminal proceedings concerning juveniles: the order commits a child to the care of the local authority. Thereafter, the local authority has the responsibility of deciding whether the child should be placed in a community home or other residential establishment, boarded out with foster parents or returned to his own home. Community homes range from community homes with education on the premises (the former approved schools) to small community-based children's homes. Unless discharged by a court, the order continues to have effect until the child reaches the age of 18, or 19 if he or she was already 16 when it was made. In criminal proceedings, which are our concern in this report, the intention of courts making care orders is usually that the offender should be removed from home.

163. In 1979, 4,552 care orders were made on juvenile offenders in criminal proceedings, which represents a significant fall from the 1971 figure of 7,499. Despite this fall, the number of young people in community homes at any one time who are subject to care orders made in criminal proceedings is four times the daily number of juveniles in borstals and detention centres. On 31 March 1979, 6,700 young offenders were resident in community homes: this compares with 1,563 juveniles in borstals and detention centres on 30 June 1979 and 1,688 on 30 June 1980. Whereas most juveniles serving detention centre sentences spend about six weeks in custody (a three month sentence with eligibility for half remission) and boys sentenced to borstal training spend an average of nine months in custody, the available evidence indicates that most children in care as a result of a criminal offence who are placed in community homes with education remain there for rather over a year.

164. It is clear from a growing body of research evidence that many of the young offenders committed to residential establishments have received care orders which are inappropriate to their circumstances. Much of this evidence has been collected by David Thorpe and his colleagues at Lancaster University. For example, in a report analysing the care orders made under Section 7 of the 1969 Children and Young Persons Act in Oldham, Thorpe measured each one against a set of criteria which demonstrated the need for residential care. The questions he asked were:

1. Is the child a danger to himself or to the community?

2. Does he have any special needs, educational, medical or otherwise, which can only be met in a residential setting?

3. Is he without a home and family in the community which can, with appropriate support, provide an adequate degree of care and control?

42

Of 132 children, only 13 satisfied one or more of these criteria. 119 (90 per cent) did not require residential care, there being no reason why they should not live in the community. A third of the children had no previous court appearances. 99 (82.2 per cent) of the care orders had been recommended to the courts by the local authority, either by the child's social worker or by an observation and assessment centre or both.

165. In Wakefield, Thorpe studied 45 children from the authority who were resident in a CHE following a care order under section 7 (7) of the 1969 Act: only nine met one or more of his criteria for residential care. Thorpe and his colleagues also recently examined the cases of 44 young offenders given care orders in Basildon, finding that 31 (70.5 per cent) of them failed to meet any of the three criteria for residential care. A third of the care orders had been imposed on the juveniles' first court appearances. In all but six of these 31 cases, the recommendations of field or residential social workers were consistent with the imposition of a care order. Similarly, a study by Buckinghamshire Social Services Department using similar criteria found that 22 of 23 young people given care orders were not in need of residential care.

166. A study by Thorpe and his colleagues of young offenders from three authorities who received inappropriate care orders found that 32.5 per cent had no previous court sentences, 28.5 per cent had one and 23.4 per cent had two. Over three quarters therefore had two or fewer previous court appearances. (Following these surveys, the authorities concerned have adopted measures designed to reduce the number of care orders made on young offenders and to develop intermediate treatment programmes for those who would previously have received care orders inappropriately).

167. While these findings are based on small samples from a few areas, national data show that 40 per cent of the care orders imposed on young offenders in 1977 were made on first offenders (Criminal Statistics, England and Wales, 1978, table 10.4). In a study of 497 young offenders committed to care in July 1975, Pat Cawson of the DHSS found that nearly 60 per cent had been given care orders on their first or second court appearance for an offence ("Young Offenders in Care, Preliminary Report", 1978).

168. The present use of care orders in criminal proceedings has disturbed several of the organisations which have given evidence to us. For example, the Conference of Chief Probation Officers suggested in its comments on the White Paper that there is "considerable evidence that care orders are made too readily". Similarly, the British Association of Social Workers stated that "a large number of children are being made the subject of a care order through the criminal process when this is unnecessary either in the interests of the child or the public". As Pat Cawson asked in her report:

> "If many children are still being prosecuted and removed from home at the first sign of delinquency, or for very trivial offences . . . . if they are still to a large extent being placed in the former approved schools and remand homes, and by all indications often spending longer periods in those establishments at an earlier age . . . . then what has happened to key sections of the 1969 Act?"

169. When a young offender is given a care order and removed to a community home for reasons connected with his own welfare following a court appearance for a minor offence, he is likely to feel aggrieved at receiving apparently harsher treatment than a similar offender from a better home background who receives a fine, a conditional discharge or a supervision order. The injustice is compounded by the fact that, if he subsequently appears in court for a further offence, he is more likely to receive a custodial sentence on the later occasion than the offender who is not yet subject to a care order.

170. While statistics for those leaving community homes with education are no longer kept, it is worth recalling that on average 66% of those leaving approved schools in the years 1963-7 were reconvicted within three years of release. There is no reason to think that reconviction rates are likely to have dropped since then, and there is some research which suggests that they may have increased. Home Office Research Study No. 32, "Residential Treatment and its Effects on Delinquency" (1975), assessed the results of work undertaken at Kingswood CHE in Bristol. The research, which spanned the period 1965-73, was undertaken in two of the school's house units, one providing intervention along "therapeutic community" lines and another offering a more conventional approved school approach. The percentage of boys reconvicted within two years of leaving the two houses were 70 per cent and 69 per cent respectively, while those leaving a third house at Kingswood had a 68 per cent reconviction rate, and the researchers suggested that even these figures probably under-estimated the real position. For example, of the 87 successes, 30 were known to have committed offences after the two year follow-up period chosen for the research.

171. More recently, in their report "Punishment and Welfare" (University of Lancaster, 1979), Thorpe, Green and Smith examined the subsequent behaviour of young offenders from Rochdale sent to community homes with education and found that two thirds had been reconvicted at least once following their first CHE placement. The authors commented that these figures were more or less in line with previous studies "and may actually be worse, since they relate to a shorter period subsequent to discharge from a CHE than the two years to which reconviction data usually refer."

172. Moreover, studies have shown that many of those sent to community homes commit further offences during their stay in the institution. In Michael Zander's study, "What Happens to Young Offenders in Care?" (New Society, 24th July 1975), further offences were committed by 67 of the 102 young offenders given care orders who were sent to institutions away from home. Similarly, the DHSS report by Pat Cawson which looked at 497 young offenders committed to care in July 1975 found that 177 of these young people were reported to have committed further offences in the nine months immediately after the care order: two-thirds of them were in residential care at the time of re-offending.

173. In summary, the evidence suggests a readiness on the part of social workers to recommend and the courts to impose care orders at an early stage on many young offenders for whom residential care is apparently unnecessary.

Residential care orders

174. The Magistrates' Association in its observations of May 1980 on the Children and Young Persons Act criticised the present position whereby the local authority to whose care the child is committed has the responsibility of deciding where he or she should be placed:

> "Many instances have been recorded where juveniles have in fact been allowed by administrative decision to return home the same day as the order of the court, either because no place could be found in a community home willing to take the child or even because the local authority disagreed with the court's decision."

175. The available evidence in fact suggests that local authorities and the courts do not often disagree about the placement of a young offender under a care order. In Zander's study 101 out of 224 young offenders given care orders were sent home — but only in 39 cases was this because assessment centres and social workers thought that was the best thing for them. 62 went home because there was nowhere else for them to go. In Cawson's survey half the home placements were due to lack of an immediate vacancy, and in only 18 per cent of the first home placements was the child sent home because this was felt to be the best thing for him or her.

176. The joint working party of the Magistrates' Association and the local authority associations which reported in July 1978 agreed on guidelines designed to ensure that local authorities meet the expectations of the courts that in certain circumstances a juvenile offender would be removed from home. The Magistrates' Association has acknowledged that these "have gone some way to dealing with the problem" but nevertheless considers that "the position appears to be far from satisfactory." The Association has therefore proposed that courts be empowered to make a residential care order in respect of someone who is already the subject of a care order and commits further serious offences. The Justices' Clerks' Society in its paper on child law reform of May 1980 also argued that courts be given the power to make a residential care order "in respect of the exceptionally difficult child."

177. The White Paper proposed that courts should be able to make a residential care order for a period of up to six months on a young offender who is already the subject of a care order made in criminal proceedings or in care proceedings brought on the ground that he was guilty of an offence and who is found guilty of a further imprisonable offence. An offer of legal representation will be required and the court must be satisfied that no other method of dealing with the offender is appropriate. Provided the offender is removed from home, it will be for the local authority to decide where he or she is placed — for example, in a community home, voluntary home or special school, or in foster care. The Government estimates that this will affect in the region of 500 to 900 additional children requiring placement away from home each year, including some who would otherwise have received custodial sentences.

178. The Association of Metropolitan Authorities estimates that the annual cost of the order will be at least £5 million (expenditure which it argues cannot be justified). The Association of County Councils told us that "provision must be

made for something of the order of an extra 1,000 juveniles in residential care each year" and also put the extra cost to local authorities at £5 million. In a Parliamentary answer of 15 December 1980, Sir George Young M.P. acknowledged that this estimate is "probably not far off the mark."

179. In its comments on the White Paper, the Association of Directors of Social Services opposed the residential care order on the following grounds:

(i)   The effectiveness of more residential care has not been demonstrated.

(ii)   The intervention of the courts in the allocation of scarce resources will make their use more arbitrary.

(iii)   The order may give rise to unjustified expectations on the part of offending juveniles, as the minimum period of residential care imposed by the residential care order may well be less than the period for which the care authority would require the juvenile to live away from home.

The Association also argued that, if the resources to be devoted to the residential care order were utilised in the community, this "could result in much more effective methods of dealing with juvenile delinquency."

180. The British Association of Social Workers and New Approaches to Juvenile Crime also argue that the additional cost of the residential care order would be better invested in the development of intermediate treatment. BASW points to the danger of linking determinate with indeterminate sentences:

"A child sent under a residential care order to a CH(E) and who is retained there once the residential care order has expired under the presently existing care order may wonder what has happened to the authority of the court or to natural justice."

The Association of Community Homes, also emphasised in its comments on the White Paper that the treatment of children subject to both determinate and indeterminate sentences "cannot be viable in the same establishment without each treatment plan seriously undermining the other."

181. The Residential Care Association in its comments on the White Paper suggested that the residential care order will result in "confusion, uncertainty and in certain cases unfairness'. The Association argued that, although the Government has stressed that a residential care order is not analogous to a custodial sentence, young people will not view this in a similar light; that non-offenders will feel a sense of injustice at having to remain in residential care until they are 18, compared with children subject to residential care orders who could be discharged after six months even though they have broken the law; and that the order will further accentuate public assumptions that all children in care are offenders.

182. While opposing the residential care order, New Approaches to Juvenile Crime nevertheless deprecates the practice of recommending or imposing care orders in cases where there is no immediate intention to remove the child from home. Its memorandum to the Secretary of State for Social Services and the Home Secretary of March 1980 noted with concern the tendency for some social workers to suggest care orders in cases where it is not intended to remove the

child from home but as a safeguard should he or she fail to respond to supervision in the community, and observed that, in other cases where social workers recommend a supervision order, magistrates may make a care order while specifically stating that they intend the child should remain home on trial. New Approaches argued that this is "a totally inappropriate use of the care order" and that a supervision order would be the correct course. It suggested that guidance along these lines should be given to courts in an explanatory circular, perhaps issued on the passing of any future legislation concerning juvenile offenders.

The removal of care orders from criminal proceedings
183. In our view, the problems which have given rise to the unsatisfactory residential care order proposal are a reflection of the essential inappropriateness of incorporating a welfare-based system of care orders into criminal proceedings. A particularly cogent argument against the present position was developed by Mr Brian Harris, Clerk to the Justices at Poole Magistrates' Court, in a recent edition of "Family Law" (1978, No. 3). He pointed out that a ten year old child who commits a minor offence can find himself the subject of an order which could take him away from his parents for the next eight years, "not because anyone believes that this is the punishment appropriate to that offence, but because the bench have been persuaded that this course is in the child's best interests."

184. Aruging that this results in a sense of injustice among parents and children, Mr Harris commented:

"If a child is brought before the court in care proceedings social workers, teachers and other witnesses will be called to give evidence on oath and what they have to say will be fully disclosed to the child and his parents, who will have the opportunity to cross-examine the applicant's witnesses and of calling witnesses of their own. By contrast, the determination of 'sentence' in criminal proceedings is a very cursory affair . . . a child who is made the subject of a criminal charge can be taken away from his home on a care order 'for his own good' without any of the safeguards that Parliament has seen fit to lay down for care proceedings where the child's welfare is the sole consideration."

He recommended the removal from the juvenile court of the power to make a care order in criminal proceedings and proposed that care proceedings should be transferred to the new domestic court. We are persuaded by this argument, which coincides with the views expressed to us by the Justices' Clerks' Society, Justice for Children and the National Council for Civil Liberties.

185. The Black Report on legislation and services for children and young persons in Northern Ireland recommended that care orders should not be available to the juvenile court when it is dealing with criminal cases. It proposed that, except in the case of very serious offences, all existing custodial and residential orders for juveniles should be amalgamated into a single determinate sentence with a maximum period of two years and a minimum period of one month. This would be subject to half remission and would be reduced by the time spent in custody on remand. Courts would thereby be given the opportunity "of fixing the period to be spent in custody in accordance with their assessment of the

gravity of the offence and the potential danger to society, rather than leaving release dates to be settled by others according to different criteria" (para. 6.29). This order would be used "sparingly and only in particularly serious or harmful cases". The Committee envisaged a single mixed secure establishment for this purpose with a regime "as helpful and supportive as possible". Juveniles of compulsory school age would receive education, older children would receive vocational training, and recreational and other social activities would be provided.

186. Announcing the Government's acceptance of these proposals to the House of Commons Northern Ireland Committee on 5 November 1980, Mr Michael Alison M.P., Minister of State, estimated that of the 200 young offenders currently in Northern Ireland's training schools nearly half did not need to be in a custodial or residential establishment in terms of the gravity of their offences. He stated that in future "only the more serious offender, against whom society needs protection, would be removed from home and taken into the residential institution", which will be run by former training school staff rather than prison officers. Mr Alison pointed out that, as a result of these changes, Northern Ireland will be one of the first areas in Europe which will no longer accommodate any children in adult penal establishments.

187. We are strongly attracted by this approach which combines a clearly understood element of punishment for serious or persistent young offenders with the safeguards of determinacy and a determined effort to reduce the number of young offenders committed to institutional care. **We recommend that care orders should no longer be an available option in criminal proceedings, but should be replaced by a new determinate residential order designed for a small minority of persistent or serious young offenders who require an element of punishment (represented by loss of liberty, not by a harsh or negative regime) and secure containment.**

188. Under such an order, offenders would be committed to one of a number of establishments which, as in Northern Ireland, should be staffed by residential workers, not prison officers, with a regime which includes well developed facilities for vocational training, education, counselling and the development of social skills. It may be appropriate for some establishments to cater for children serving short term sentences, while others develop a regime appropriate for those receiving longer sentences. We acknowledge that for some young people (offenders and non-offenders) removal from home is necessary because of the damaging effect on them of life within the families concerned. Any young offender for whom committal to the care of the local authority was considered essential on such strictly welfare-oriented grounds could of course still receive such a disposal if civil care proceedings were instituted.

Safeguards
189. We recognise that such a fundamental change is unlikely to be introduced without full consultation and careful planning. In the short term, we therefore favour the implementation of measures which would increase the safeguards for the potential and actual recipients of care orders in criminal proceedings.

190. The Magistrates' Association, the Justices Clerks' Society and New Approaches to Juvenile Crime all consider that an offer of legal representation should

be mandatory before a care order is made. At present, a juvenile cannot be committed to a junior detention centre for what is now in practice a six week term without being offered legal representation; yet under a care order a young person can be removed from home and sent to an institution for a considerably longer period. Legal representation can help to ensure that the proceedings are clarified for the juvenile; that full enquiries are made to ensure that the prosecution's presentation of the facts is accurate and the juvenile has been able to make a sound and considered judgement as to his plea; that the juvenile's views are properly heard; that there is a clear presentation of mitigating circumstances; that social work and other professional reports can be scrutinised for inaccuracies and challenged if necessary; and that advice on appeal is given. Legal representation is desirable for parents as well as children: where the parents are separated, each might need separate representation.

191. **We recommend that an offer of legal representation for the child and his or her parents should be mandatory before a care order is made.**

192. The Magistrates' Association also proposed in its comments of May 1980 that there should be a judicial review of care cases and argued:

"In the case of, for example, psychiatric patients detained against their will, periodic appeal is possible to the Mental Health Review Tribunal, but the sane child enjoys no such privilege. Reviews are admittedly undertaken by the local authority every six months but they appear to be of a very cursory nature . . . We do not know of any local authority which holds a formal review where the child is legally represented or where his views are expressed."

193. Similar views are expressed by New Approaches to Juvenile Crime which proposes that local authorities should be asked to make arrangements for regular review of the position of a young offender subject to a care order by a body which includes some element of lay involvement. The juvenile, his or her parents and where appropriate foster parents would have the right to appear and speak before this body, "whose lay members might appropriately be representatives of the magistracy". The Howard League for Penal Reform proposed in its comments on the Green Paper that the juvenile court should review each care order every six months. We note that in Scotland a supervision order with a residential requirement (the nearest equivalent to the care order) lapses after a year unless it is reviewed by the children's panel.

194. **We recommend that the position of a young offender subject to a care order should be regularly reviewed by a body including one or more members of the juvenile bench before which the child, his parents and foster parents where appropriate should have the right to appear.**

195. New Approaches to Juvenile Crime proposes that a care order should only be recommended if a child has certain educational, vocational, medical or personal needs which can best be met in a residential establishment or a foster home; the home circumstances of the child are such that more severe emotional damage or behavioural disorders would result if he or she were allowed to remain at home; or the behaviour of the child is a positive danger to himself, to the community or both. It suggests also that when a recommendation for a care

order (or custodial sentence) is contained in a report by a social worker or probation officer, the court should ask the social services or probation service what alternatives have been considered. The argument for such a policy is underlined by a recent review of social enquiry reports on juveniles which was carried out by a joint Working Party of the Devon Probation and After-Care Service and Social Services Department. The Working Party considered 147 reports presented to the courts between 1st October 1978 and 31st March 1979 which had recommended supervision, detention centre, borstal or care orders. Recommendations to the court were present in almost every report reviewed; yet, although in 34 per cent the recommendation was for custody or residential care, in less than a third of this latter group of cases had the social worker or probation officer first considered a community based alternative.

196. **We recommend that more precise criteria for the making of care orders in criminal proceedings should be laid down by statute or by guidance to courts and local authorities.** These should provide that care orders should only be recommended or made where it is the intention that the child should immediately be removed from home, and this should be based on strict criteria concerning the needs of the child and the threat he or she poses to the community. **We further recommend that, when a recommendation for a care order is contained in a report by a social worker or probation officer, the court should ask the social services or probation service what alternatives have been considered.**

Observation and Assessment Centres

197. Following the 1969 Children and Young Persons Act, observation and assessment centres replaced the former classifying schools, reception centres and remand homes. Section 36 of the Act requires each region to provide facilities "for the observation of the physical and mental condition of children in the care of the relevant authorities and for the assessment of the most suitable accommodation and treatment for those children." The centres provide information about the backgrounds and characteristics of the young people concerned to the juvenile court and also to the local authorities to assist their decisions concerning treatment and placement. On 31 March 1979, there were 4,845 children in observation and assessment centres in England and Wales, of whom 1,376 were offenders.

198. In recent years there has been considerable questioning of the usefulness of the practice of observing and assessing children in residential observation and assessment centres away from their homes, families and usual surroundings. A child's behaviour can change considerably when he enters an observation and assessment centre where he may not manifest the same problems which he has in adjusting to his home or school environment. There is also evidence suggesting that residential assessment biases reports towards recommending a further residential placement.

199. A seminar held jointly by the DHSS Social Work Service and the Association of Directors of Social Services in January 1977 concluded that considerably greater emphasis should be placed on non-residential observation and assessment, while acknowledging that residential assessment was essential in some cases. The report of the seminar stated:

"A general principle might be that assessment should be carried out in the child's home setting wherever possible. Exceptionally assessment should be carried out in a special place on a day basis . . . Very exceptionally assessment should take place in a residential setting."

200. It suggested that existing observation and assessment centres should be replaced by an observation and assessment service within the local authority, involving a "comprehensive domiciliary/day/residential approach to observing and assessing children by a multi-disciplinary team of skilled staff". Those involved in such a separate service might include specialists from the disciplines of educational psychology, psychiatry, paediatrics and social work. The Magistrates' Association expressed similar views in a recent memorandum submitted to the DHSS Working Party on Observation and Assessment, in which it argued that an observation and assessment service should be provided "without removing the child from home unless absolutely necessary" and stated:

"The need for a multi-disciplinary approach to assessment is recognised. This in itself may be a costly provision but it would be even more costly in a residential setting. Better use could be made of existing child guidance clinics for the assessment of children who need not be removed from home. In some instances more Observation and Assessment Centres might be used on a day basis."

The Association conceded that a minority of children cannot be assessed adequately in their own homes and advocated residential provision for those children requiring assessment away from home "for their own protection or that of society."

201. The Association of Directors of Social Services in its submission to the DHSS Working Party on Observation and Assessment pointed out that observation and assessment centres are the social services' most expensive residential resource apart from community homes with education and recommended that "every encouragement be given to a wider use of non-residential assessment procedures." It is important that local authorities and other social agencies should not compartmentalise the notion of observation and assessment: assessment should start the moment a child and his or her family comes into contact with a helping agency. Many children coming into care are already well known to the Social Services Department or to other agencies. "First Year At Fairfield Lodge" (1976), a study by Hampshire's Social Services Research and Intelligence Unit, found that 68 per cent of the children in Fairfield Lodge observation and assessment centre had been subject to some form of children's legislation before admission. Similarly, a study carried out in 1975 and 1976 by the South West Children's Regional Planning Committee of children's progress through the region's observation and assessment centres found that the majority of children had had experience of some form of treatment or care before admission to the centre, and most of these experiences had occurred in the fairly recent past. A survey by the DHSS Social Work Service in 1976 of 102 assessment centres showed that 29 per cent of the children in them had previously been subject to supervision orders and, in one particular region, 35 per cent of the children had been seen at child guidance centres (though not always recently). In such cases, a

further separate programme of observation and assessment in a residential centre divorced from the child's home environment is of questionable usefulness.

202. Local authorities require emergency reception and short-stay centres for children, accommodation for juveniles on remand who have not been granted bail and holding centres for children awaiting a long term placement (though these functions do not necessarily have to be carried out by an observation and assessment centre). There is a growing consensus, however, that assessment as such is best done on a non-residential basis whenever possible, and should preferably include observation and assessment in the family home. Many areas are developing forms of day attendance at a centre or clinic. In appropriate cases, assessment can be combined with forms of intervention: Maynard House Observation and Assessment Centre, Barnet, provides an example of an approach which combines a domiciliary assessment service with intermediate treatment (including weekend residence at Maynard House) for children who need this form of intervention.

203. We are grateful to the Secretary of State for Social Services for allowing us to see the report of the DHSS Working Party on Observation and Assessment in advance of publication, and we have been encouraged by the degree of similarity between the Working Party's approach and our own. The development of non-residential assessment was warmly endorsed in the evidence which the working party received from social workers, residential staff, magistrates and professional associations representing psychologists, general practitioners, nurses, child and adolescent and forensic psychiatrists. It commented:

"With such support and enthusiasm for the theory of non-residential assessments we found ourselves asking why there was so little in practice."

204. We strongly support the working party's view that "there should be a significant and steady shift of emphasis away from residential assessment"; its recommendation that a child who does not need to be in residential care should not be admitted to a home solely for the purpose of being assessed; and its proposal that there should be a considerable reduction in the number of residential assessment places, beginning with a 30 per cent reduction over the next four years.

205. **We recommend that there should be a shift of emphasis and resources from residential observation and assessment towards non-residential assessment, including observation and assessment in the family home wherever possible. Better use should be made of child guidance clinics for the assessment of children who need not be removed from home. We further recommend that in appropriate cases an assessment period should be used as an opportunity for positive assistance to the child and the family.**

Secure accommodation

206. An increasing number of children given care orders are spending some time in secure accommodation. In England and Wales there are now 494 secure places in existence, and a further 155 places are under construction. Such units are very expensive, partly because of the special building requirements and partly because of the high staff ratios needed to operate them: the average capital cost of a secure place is about £26,000 and to keep a child in a secure place for a year costs anything between £14,100 and £33,800.

207. There have been two major research studies on secure units — the Dartington Social Research Unit's Study "Locking Up Children" (1978) by Spencer Millham, Roger Bullock and Kenneth Hosie and "Children Referred to Closed Units" (DHSS Research Report No. 5, 1979) by Pat Cawson and Mary Martell. These studies show that secure units are currently being used for younger and less delinquent children than was the case several years ago and that their reconviction rates are high.

208. The Dartington Unit found that boys currently in secure units were less delinquent and less institutionalised than admissions in earlier years: in 1975 only 38 per cent were over 14½ compared with 65 per cent in 1971. The report found that secure units confer some benefits on children, breaking the persistent absconding patterns and extreme withdrawal of some neurotic children, and conferring physical and educational advantages on them. Nevertheless, of 587 boys released from secure units and followed up for two years, 76 per cent of those released to the community re-offended. The majority then underwent a further spell in an institution, usually a borstal. The authors observed:

"For the majority of boys the secure units provide a brief sojourn in an expensive ante-room to the penal system."

209. The DHSS study, which concerned children referred to secure units at Kingswood, Redhill, Red Bank and St. Charles youth treatment centre from 1971-74, produced similar findings. It found that the children referred were younger than those admitted to the units before 1971, two-thirds of the referrals being 13 or 14 year olds, and suggested that the age range was probably accounted for by the rise in committal of juveniles to borstal in recent years. The figures implied that it was not refusal or lack of availability of secure places which had led to the increased committal of older boys to borstal, since so few were even referred to secure facilities in the child care service: almost all the children referred were too young for borstal admission.

210. The children had less serious offence histories (i.e. fewer court appearances and at a younger age) than earlier admissions to secure units. Few had been convicted of violent offences and a fifth had never appeared in court charged with an offence. The results suggested that boys being referred to secure units were considerably less delinquent than the intake of the units before the implementation of the 1969 Act, while the girls were apparently less delinquent than the former admissions to girls' approved schools.

211. Of the sample of 40 children whose subsequent progress was followed up by the researchers, 78 per cent reoffended within the year following discharge: 40 per cent of them committed six or more offences during this one year period. The researchers concluded:

" . . . present indications are that admission to the units increases the probability of subsequent offending for younger children and non-offenders or less serious offenders . . . Children admitted to the units had in some respects a poorer record after discharge than would have been expected from their previous records, which may indicate a criminogenic effect of admission to a unit, particularly in the younger and less criminally sophisticated . . . there are clear indications that the trend towards admitting younger and less delinquent children to closed units is a dangerous one which should be reconsidered."

212. The report of a working party of the Howard League for Penal Reform, " ' Unruly' Children in a Human Context" (1977), proposed detailed criteria which should be met before a secure placement is permissible. It also argued that, while decisions as to short term placement for up to two months in secure accommodation should be made by a senior local authority officer under the terms of the existing care order, after that period such a placement should be reviewed by a panel composed of elected members of the care authority, together with an independent person, and further confirmed or rejected by the juvenile court bench sitting in court: the child should be legally represented and aided. The report proposed that this review and confirmation should take place at the end of the first two months and then at six monthly intervals thereafter, and that the three monthly review required by the community homes regulations should carry on alongside this procedure. The latter review must be carried out on a young person in secure accommodation at three monthly intervals by a review committee including one independent person. The report acknowledges that its proposals would be cumbersome, but argues that this machinery is "essential . . . to ensure that all these interests participate in a solemn decision of this kind."

213. The report of the DHSS Working Party on "Legal and Professional Aspects of the use of Secure Accommodation for Children in Care" (1981) recommended that secure accommodation should be reserved for "those children whose behaviour has demonstrated that the risks to themselves and/or society are too great for alternative forms of care to be appropriate." Commenting that the three monthly review required by the community homes regulations "can become an administrative formality", the working party proposed that there should be a right of application to the courts regarding a decision at a review to confirm the detention of a child in secure accommodation. We share the concern that adequate safeguards for children in secure accommodation must be developed, and we would prefer to see the simple safeguard of a regular review of the juvenile court rather than a cumbersome and possibly slow-moving review machinery of the kind proposed by the Howard League working party.

214. **We recommend that criteria for the use of secure accommodation should be incorporated in statutory regulations.** These might make the detention of a young person in secure accommodation conditional on such criteria as the existence of a major risk to the public because the child is likely to commit a serious offence; that the child would not stay unless kept securely as evidenced, for example, by previous persistent absconding; or that the child's behaviour threatens staff, other residents or himself and only a secure unit has the capacity to deal with him. **We further recommend that any decision by a three-monthly review committee to continue the detention of a young person in secure accommodation should be subject to confirmation by the juvenile court. An offer of legal representation for the child at the court hearing should be mandatory.**

Summary of recommendations

1. Care orders should no longer be an available option in criminal proceedings, but should be replaced by a new determinate residential order designed for a small minority of persistent or serious young offenders who require an element of punishment (represented by loss of liberty, not by a harsh or negative regime) and secure containment (para. 187).

2. In the short term:

   (i) An offer of legal representation for the child and his or her parents should be mandatory before a care order is made (para. 191).

   (ii) The position of a young offender subject to a care order should be regularly reviewed by a body including one or more members of the juvenile bench before which the child, his parents and foster parents where appropriate should have the right to appear (para. 194).

   (iii) More precise criteria for the making of care orders in criminal proceedings should be laid down by statute or by guidance to courts and local authorities (para. 196).

   (iv) When a recommendation for a care order is contained in a report by a social worker or probation officer, the court should ask the social services or probation service what alternatives have been considered (para. 196).

3. There should be a shift of emphasis and resources from residential observation and assessment towards non-residential assessment, including observation and assessment in the family home wherever possible. Better use should be made of child guidance clinics for the assessment of children who need not be removed from home (para. 205).

4. In appropriate cases an assessment period should be used as an opportunity for positive assistance to the child and the family (para. 205).

5. Criteria for the use of secure accommodation should be incorporated in statutory regulations (para. 214).

6. Any decision by a three-monthly review committee to continue the detention of a young person in secure accommodation should be subject to confirmation by the juvenile court. An offer of legal representation for the child at the court hearing should be mandatory (para. 214).

215. Offenders under 21 are currently eligible for three different custodial sentences. Those aged 17 or over may receive prison sentences which, as in the case of adult offenders, are subject to remission of one third of the sentence which may be forfeited for disciplinary offences. Those aged 15 and under 21 are eligible for sentences of borstal training, which require their detention in custody for a minimum of six months and a maximum of two years. The court does not stipulate the period of training: release is authorised by the Home Secretary in each case on the basis of a recommendation from the Board of Visitors of the establishment concerned. Offenders aged 14 and under 21 may be sentenced to detention in a detention centre for a minimum term of three months and a maximum of six months, the majority of sentences being for three months. Offenders sentenced to detention are eligible for remission of one third of the sentence, and for half the sentence in the case of juveniles.

Youth custody
216. We consider the present distinction between young prisoner accommodation and borstal establishments to be unnecessarily rigid, particularly since overcrowding in one part of the custodial system cannot readily be relieved by using vacancies in another part. We also share the White Paper's view that, except in the special circumstances of the life sentence, all sentences should be determinate "so that courts can mark the seriousness of the offence by the length of the sentence they impose" (para. 11). The White Paper proposes to amalgamate imprisonment and borstal training into a determinate "youth custody" sentence, the length of which will be decided by the courts in each individual case, subject to the maximum period of imprisonment which would be applicable to an adult.

217. All young adults given a custodial sentence of over 4 months will be sentenced to youth custody and "will serve their sentence in much the same kind of accommodation as at present, ie a borstal, a young prisoner centre, or a young prisoners' wing or other accommodation in an adult prison" (para. 18). The intention is that all young adult offenders receiving short to medium term sentences of youth custody will be guaranteed a place in a training establishment. Those receiving longer sentences will be placed in training establishments as far as vacancies permit, but no individual will be guaranteed a place. The Government hopes to increase the proportion of training places "in the long term and as resources allow" (para. 21). The length of sentence below which a training place will be guaranteed will be fixed in legislation with the provision that any alteration to it shall be made by means of an order approved by Parliament. It is proposed that, in the first place, the dividing line will be eighteen monťhs, but "this may need to be adjusted in the light of experience". We return to the question of training regimes later in this chapter.

218. The proposed introduction of determinacy into all custodial sentences for this age group will be widely welcomed. As the Prison and Borstal Governors' Branch of the Society of Civil and Public Servants said in its comments on the Green Paper of 1978:

> "The indeterminacy of the present Borstal sentence has been used more for administrative convenience in solving overcrowding problems than it has in meeting the needs of trainees. In addition, experience and research indicate that performance in an institution bears little relationship to performance in the outside world . . . The arbitrariness of the system from the trainee's perspective is clearly exemplified by the different target dates operative in different institutions. Time spent in custody can thus be dependent on the vagaries of the allocation procedure rather than on any individual effort."

219. One beneficial effect of the new youth custody sentence would be the repeal of Section 3 of the Criminal Justice Act 1961, which provides that, with certain exceptions, a court wishing to pass a custodial sentence of more than six months but less than three years on a young adult must pass the indeterminate sentence of borstal training. As the White Paper points out, this has "deprived the courts of their power, within the range of six months to three years, of imposing a determinate sentence whose length was appropriate to the circumstances of the particular offence and the young offender" (para. 10). The Magistrates' Association argued in its comments on the last Government's Green Paper that the removal of this provision "in the interest of justice is long overdue"

220. The Advisory Council on the Penal System in its report on "Young Adult Offenders" (1974) suggested that these restrictions may have increased the periods which young adults spend in custody in two ways. First, many young males receiving borstal sentences and now spending about nine months in custody would otherwise have received prison sentences of nine months (in effect six months with full remission) or one year (eight months with full remission). Among adult prisoners received into custody over the six months level, sentences of up to twelve months are the most numerous, and the Advisory Council suggested that, if the courts had complete discretion in the length of sentence, there is no reason to believe that the pattern of sentences they would impose on young adults would be significantly different from that for adults.

221. Secondly, there is reason to believe that courts occasionally impose sentences of three years' imprisonment in cases where, but for the restrictions, they would have given the offender, say, 2 or 2½ years. While the section has also had the opposite effect in other cases, as some young adults have been sentenced to borstal training in circumstances likely to have attracted substantial prison sentences in the case of an adult, it is indefensible that some offenders should receive artificially short sentences at the expense of others receiving unnecessarily long ones.

222. **We recommend that borstal training and imprisonment for young adults should be combined into a single determinate sentence of youth custody.**

223. In principle, combining the two sentences should make it possible to allocate more offenders to places near their homes, thereby making it easier for relatives, friends, probation officers and social workers to visit them. However, the scope for this will be reduced considerably if allocation to establishments is to be based primarily on the length of sentence.NACRO argued in its comments on the White Paper that the consideration of nearness to home and family should normally take precedence over other placing considerations. The Howard League for Penal Reform argued in its comments on the Green Paper that those serving longer sentences should be given priority in being placed near their homes:

"family relationships may stand the strain of a short placement in a remote institution where visiting is difficult, but if they are to survive a medium or long sentence they should not be subject to long, expensive and tiring journeys too."

224. Similarly, the National Association of Probation Officers suggested in its comments on the Green Paper that with few exceptions the first priority should be the maintenance of links between the offender, the family and workers in the community, and that only in rare cases should special needs for security, training or treatment outweigh the need to be as near home as possible. The Association questioned the need to segregate offenders by length of sentence and suggested that "the mixing of variable length of sentence gives those in the institution a greater sense of contact with the outside community."

225. We acknowledge that there is a conflict between the desirability of placing young offenders in establishments near their homes and the possible advantages of allocating a young offender to a youth custody centre with a regime geared to the needs of those serving sentences of a certain length. However, we consider that the maintenance of links with families, probation officers and voluntary associates is of such paramount importance in the resettlement of difficult young people that this consideration should normally take precedence. **We recommend that placing offenders in establishments near their homes should receive a high priority in decisions concerning the allocation of offenders between youth custody centres.**

The mentally unfit
226. The White Paper proposes that most young adults receiving sentences of four months or less will not be eligible for youth custody. They will receive detention centre sentences unless they are considered physically or mentally unfit, have served two previous custodial sentences or are committed to custody in default of a money payment ordered by a court, or an order is made to the contrary by the court for any other special reason to be entered in the record of the proceedings:

"These young adults will be sentenced to youth custody but placed as appropriate by the prison department. They are most likely to serve their sentences in accommodation in adult prisons in much the same way as young adults who are currently sentenced to up to six months in prison" (para. 17).

We regard this as extremely disturbing, particularly so far as the mentally unfit are concerned: serving a sentence in an adult prison can hardly be described as "appropriate" for such offenders, though it may be administratively convenient.

227. **We recommend that those offenders for whom a custodial sentence exceeding four months is inappropriate but who are mentally unfit for detention centre regimes should not receive any form of custodial sentence.** Since these are cases where by definition only a short sentence is being considered, the offenders concerned will not be among those who represent the most serious danger to the community and a suitable non-custodial sentence, where appropriate involving treatment for the offender's mental condition within the National Health Service, should be imposed.

228. We acknowledge, following our recent discussions with the DHSS, that the Department is making considerable efforts to ensure that mentally disordered offenders can be dealt with within the National Health Service or in hostels and other community-based facilities rather than in prison department custody. We are nevertheless compelled to re-state our view that the detention of mentally disordered people in prison department establishments is a serious blot on our society which should be removed forthwith. However, since past experience suggests that this aim is unlikely to be achieved in the immediate future, we are obliged with some reluctance to make a further recommendation taking account of this probability. **We recommend that, when custodial sentences are imposed on mentally ill or disordered young offenders, the Prison Department should ensure that these are served in establishments or units which are geared as far as possible to the special needs of such offenders.** We have no precise estimates of the number of young offenders likely to fall into this category and we cannot therefore make a firm recommendation concerning the number of such establishments or units which might be required; but as a minimum there should be one such establishment or unit for the south and one for the north of England.

229. In our report "Too Many Prisoners" we recommended that Governors should be empowered to apply for variation of a custodial sentence to a panel of magistrates. This proposal was designed in particular to enable prisoners whose primary reason for offending is a mental disorder or addiction to alcohol or drugs to be removed from prison department custody to another more appropriate setting. This recommendation has been criticised on the grounds *inter alia* that any such application for variation of sentence should be to a court of the same status as the original sentencing court, and we acknowledge the validity of this criticism. **We recommend that Governors of establishments containing young people sentenced to youth custody should be empowered to apply to a court of the same status as the original sentencing court for variation of a youth custody sentence.**

Young women offenders
230. In 1979, the average daily number of young women in custody was 432, in comparison with a figure of 12,358 for young males. Of the 432, an average of 117 were awaiting trial or sentence, 101 were serving prison sentences and 214 were serving sentences of borstal training (47 of whom were located in local prisons and remand centres): detention centre sentences are not available for young women. Since the population of young women in custody is much smaller

than that of young men, the problem of providing appropriate facilities should yield to a determined effort to provide a solution. No such determined effort has yet been made and we consider the present arrangements for young women to be particularly unsatisfactory.

231. The White Paper proposes that the detention centre sentence will continue to be available, as at present, only for young men, and that the youth custody sentence should be available for all young women given a custodial sentence of three weeks or more. The number of establishments which could be used as youth custody centres for young women is very small: there is at present only one closed borstal and one open borstal for young women, both in the South East, in addition to small borstal units in three adult women's establishments.

232. The Howard League for Penal Reform argued in its comments on the Green Paper that the policy of having only single-sex institutions means that many relatives face exhausting journeys if they want to visit, and often find they cannot. It suggested that this is especially serious in the case of the only closed girls' borstal, Bullwood Hall, which is in south Essex but draws two thirds of its inmates from north of the Wash. The following table shows the proportion of girls discharged from Bullwood Hall in the last three years who had received no visits or only one visit from family and friends and no visits from either a probation officer or a social worker during their stay (which is on average seven months):

	1978	1979	1980
No visits from family or friends	29%	23%	13%
One visit from family or friends	20%	20%	16%
No visit from probation officer or social worker	50%	29%	29%

The inconvenient location of Bullwood Hall was one of the reasons which led the Advisory Council on the Penal System to recommend in its report of 1974 that it should "cease to be used as a borstal for young women as soon as possible" (para. 324).

233. In evidence submitted to the Expenditure Committee January 1979, the Prison and Borstal Governors' Branch pointed out that female prisoners are often located hundreds of miles away from their home areas and suggested that a number of small custodial units for women should be opened, scattered throughout the country and linked to male establishments, either as separate wings or units within existing accommodation or as satellites nearby. Both staff and inmates could then share many of the resources at present available to their male counterparts. The Branch argued:

> "There is no reason why suitable female inmates should not be able to mix with male inmates in the context of supervised work, educational classes, some recreational activities, etc. Staff would be able to share training

resources and other facilities. Many female inmates would be able to be located nearer to their home areas, with all the consequential advantages that would follow. They would be in relatively small groups in which they could feel personally known and understood and would receive individual attention. This would avoid some of the disturbed behaviour which is shown by women inmates in larger groups. There would be less stress on staff, and improved prospects for recruitment and training".

234. Similarly, the Conference of Chief Probation Officers argued in its comments on the Green Paper that female young offenders should be located as near to home as possible, not only for the development of good through-care but also to deal more effectively with the domestic problems frequently associated with female offenders of all ages. It saw it as preferable that small youth custody units for women should be provided in a range of establishments in different parts of the country. The National Association of Probation Officers, the Howard League for Penal Reform, the Magistrates' Association and NACRO expressed similar views in their comments on the Green Paper. NACRO echoed the Governors' Branch in suggesting that this development would "enable some limited association to take place between male and female offenders for the purpose of, for example, education and recreational activity", and the Howard League for Penal Reform also suggested that "young men and women should be able to meet at work and leisure during the day". In "Young Adult Offenders" the Advisory Council on the Penal System suggested that

"there may be occasions when young men and women offenders can engage in joint activities in situations which avoid artificiality, such as recreation and group work, and we do not see any argument of principle which need exclude this" (para. 325).

235. **We recommend that young adult women in custody should be located in small youth custody units attached to male establishments and opportunities should be developed for co-educational activities involving both male and female young offenders in custody.**

Regimes
236. The White Paper describes the Government's long term aim as "to extend in time to all young offenders except those serving the shortest terms a regime which is as positive and constructive as possible" but states that there is a long way to go before this can be achieved with existing resources (para. 11). It suggests that, except for those serving shorter sentences, custodial regimes for young adults

"should be modelled on the best of the borstal system, providing a range of education, work and social training which is designed to help young people on release to cope with the normal demands of modern society without reverting to crime" (para. 12).

237. The last Government's Green Paper also described its approach to custodial regimes as being "based on the best of existing practice in the borstal system". It proposed that educational activities should be related to the individual's future educational needs and employment prospects; that educa-

tional courses should be designed to prepare the offender for further educational training in the community after release to supervision; and that greater use should be made of day release courses in the community.

238. It envisaged that youth custody centres would continue to provide, as most borstals do now, for forms of personal development through group work or other schemes where the individual offender is encouraged to discuss his circumstances and his problems. The training programme in custody would be particularly related to the offenders' home needs, including courses in home maintenance, "survival training" intended to help them look after themselves in the community and courses in social skills. Direct involvement in community work would form a deliberate part of the youth custody regime. Remedial education would remain an important ingredient, as it is at present, for the large number of inmates needing it, and further education would be available where appropriate. For others the continuing emphasis on physical fitness, physical health and cleanliness would be more important. For young offenders serving medium and long term sentences, industrial work and more fully developed training and educational facilities would be provided.

239. In its comments on the Green Paper, NACRO argued that sufficient resources should be available to make these aims a reality and not mere lip service — for example, to provide courses in social skills for inmates of all institutions for young adults and to make available counselling on a voluntary "contract" basis. The National Association of Probation Officers also urged "an even greater emphasis on the teaching of social skills". The Conference of Chief Probation Officers expressed the firm belief that some young offenders in custody can be positively influenced by counselling and proposed that the establishment of priorities in training programmes should take note of this fact.

240. **We recommend that suitable training regimes should be provided for all those sentenced to youth custody. These should incorporate facilities of a high standard for work, vocational training, education and the development of social skills.**

241. NACRO argued in its comments on the Green Paper that the large scale duplication inside penal institutions of facilities which also exist in the community (e.g. education and training courses) would be unacceptably wasteful and expensive. It pointed out that at present a very small number of inmates are allowed to go out from custodial establishments to attend courses of education and training locally and suggested that this practice provides a pointer to ways in which other aspects of custodial regimes might be developed. It therefore proposed that, particularly in open institutions, the maximum use should be made of existing programmes based in the local community in which arrangements should be made for inmates to take part where possible. The National Association of Probation Officers stressed the importance of integrated courses and training, with similar programmes within the institution and in the community, so that initiatives should not be lost on release.

242. **We recommend that training for those sentenced to youth custody should be provided in conjunction with facilities in the community, and there should be more day release to outside education and training facilities. We further recomm-**

end that every encouragement should be given to young offenders to continue courses begun in youth custody centres after discharge.

243. We recognise that the provision of suitable training regimes for all young adults at present sentenced to borstal training and imprisonment would demand considerable resources and that the prospects for suitable training regimes are more limited in young prisoner wings of adult prisons than in youth custody centres. The Prison and Borstal Governors' Branch remarked in its comments on the Green Paper that

"to propose the development of regimes designed to be 'educative in the broadest sense' without acknowledging resource limitations is unrealistic in the extreme. Successive Governments have, in our view, been inclined to expect too much from the prison service for the money they have been prepared to invest, an imbalance which must be rectified by increasing available resources."

244. The current limitations on public expenditure mean that the prospects for such regimes in the near future are crucially dependent on the number of young adults sentenced to custody: if the number could be considerably reduced, the cost of providing training regimes for all those sentenced to youth custody would be less daunting than at present.

Criteria for youth custody sentences

245. In its report "Young Adult Offenders" (1974), the Advisory Council on the Penal System emphasised its wish to see "a major switch from custody to supervision in the community" (para. 48). It made a thorough review of the research on custodial sentences, concluding that, for offenders of comparable background, time spent in custody cannot be shown to produce better results than supervision in the community (para. 17). It also found that longer sentences produced no greater success rate with similar offenders than short ones, adding that some studies suggest that "reducing periods of detention improves some offenders' chances of avoiding reconviction rather than the reverse" (para. 137). It concluded:

"These considerations point in the direction of trying to achieve change not by withdrawing a person from the community but by supervising and influencing him while he remains within" (para. 158).

246. Yet in far too many cases a custodial sentence is imposed before a supervision or probation order has been tried. A Home Office study of 79 per cent of all trainees received into borstal between 1 July and 31 December 1977 revealed that over 35 per cent of those entering borstal had not received a previous supervision or probation order.

247. Section 19 of the Powers of Criminal Courts Act 1973 prohibits a court from sentencing a person aged 17 and under 21 to imprisonment unless of the opinion that no other method of dealing with him is appropriate and requires the court to take into account any available information about the offender's character and his physical and mental condition in reaching this opinion. The White Paper proposes to extend this provision to youth custody and detention centre sentences. A recent editorial in the "Criminal Law Review" (1980 Crim. L.R. p. 753) said of this proposal:

> "the Government proposes to use a formula which even its own advisers recognise to be ineffectual."

The allusion was to the comment on the same formula by Mr. M.J. Moriarty of the Home Office in oral evidence to the Expenditure Committee on 19th June 1978 that "there is not very much evidence that it has greatly affected actual sentencing practice."

248. In its comments on the Green Paper, NACRO proposed that a court in passing a custodial sentence on a young adult should be required to state that the sentence is essential for the protection of the public and to give reasons for this view. The reasons would be recorded and this part of the process would form grounds for appeal. The National Association of Probation Officers also advocated that the court should give in writing its reasons for deciding on a custodial sentence and proposed that the court should need to be satisfied that immediate custody is the only way of avoiding a serious risk to society or the offender. The Conference of Chief Probation Officers considered that, before passing a custodial sentence, courts should be expected to state what objectives the court had in mind and why those objectives could not in the court's view be achieved by the use of a non-custodial sentence. The British Association of Social Workers argued that legislation on this point must reflect the intention of using custody as a last resort and suggested a clause on the following lines:

> "An offender shall not be sentenced to a period of youth custody if a non-custodial alternative is available except where there is reason to believe that the offender would not comply with such a sentence or where it appears to the court that the person presents a sufficient risk to the public to justify containment."

249. Paragraph 3 of the White Paper contains an important statement of the Government's view of the circumstances in which custodial sentences might appropriately be imposed:

> "The Government is doing as much as possible to encourage the development of non-custodial facilities so that the courts may continue to have a range of alternatives sufficient to ensure that an offender is given a custodial or residential sentence only when he is a real danger to society, or has shown himself unwilling or unable to respond to non-custodial penalties, or, in the case of a juvenile, is in need of care and control that he is unlikely to receive at home" (para. 3).

However, the White Paper does not propose enshrining these or similar criteria in legislation.

250. **We recommend that legislation should provide that a youth custody sentence should be imposed only when the offender is a real danger to society or has shown himself unwilling or unable to respond to non-custodial penalties. A court on passing a youth custody sentence should give its reasons for this conclusion, and this part of the process should form grounds for appeal.**

Time on remand
251. At present, time spent in custody on remand does not count towards the indeterminate sentence of borstal training or the detention centre sentence. The

White Paper proposes that youth custody sentences and detention centre sentences should take account of time spent in custody on remand. This is in accordance with a recommendation of the Advisory Council on the Penal System, which stated in its report of 1974:

"Similar arrangements already apply to prison sentences, but not to sentences of detention centre and Borstal training; this is a source of grievance among young adult offenders who expect equal treatment with adults in terms of calculation of liability to custody" (para. 211).

This proposal has the support of the Magistrates' Association, the Prison and Borstal Governors' Branch, the National Association of Probation Officers, the Howard League for Penal Reform, the National Youth Bureau and NACRO.

252. The Justices' Clerks' Society, however, opposed allowing time spent in custody to count against sentence in its comments on the Green Paper, preferring to leave it to the courts to determine the appropriate sentence in the light of the time that the youth has spent in custody. It pointed out *inter alia* that a remand into the care of the local authority does not count as time spent in custody.

253. **We recommend that time spent in custody on remand should count towards a youth custody sentence. We further recommend that the courts should be asked to consider time spent on remand in local authority establishments when considering the length of a custodial sentence.**

Suspended youth custody sentences
254. There is at present a power to suspend a sentence of imprisonment imposed on an offender under 21, but not a borstal or detention centre sentence. The White Paper proposes that there should be no power to suspend sentences of detention or youth custody, in contrast to the Green Paper which proposed a power to suspend youth custody sentences and argued that "the threat of youth custody could operate as an effective and appropriate sanction for young offenders" (para. 41).

255. The present Government's view coincides with that of the Advisory Council on the Penal System in its report "Young Adult Offenders":

"If the nature of the offence is not such that the court considers an immediate custodial sentence necessary, but at the same time a considerable degree of social intervention and control over the offender's time is warranted, the court should seriously consider whether it could not use a non-custodial measure" (para. 239).

256. In its more recent report, "Sentences of Imprisonment − A Review of Maximum Penalties" (1978), the Advisory Council observed of suspended sentences of imprisonment:

"The accumulated evidence is not very encouraging. If the main object of the suspended sentence is to reduce the prison population, there are considerable doubts as to whether it has achieved this effect. It may even have increased the size of the prison population" (para. 265).

One reason for this is that the courts have in some cases misused the sanction by passing it on offenders who would not, but for the existence of the suspended sentence, have been given a custodial sentence. Courts also appear to have passed suspended sentences greater in length than the sentence of immediate imprisonment which they might otherwise have given, resulting in a longer stay in custody for the offender if the sentence is later activated in full. The Advisory Council added, however, that this is not the whole story and suggested that the number of cases in which the suspended sentence enables courts to avoid the actual imprisonment of an offender who will never incur another prison sentence, while indicating at the same time that this offence merits imprisonment, is often overlooked by those who regard the suspended sentence as a failure.

257. In its comments on the Green Paper, the Justices' Clerks' Society opposed the application of suspended sentences to young offenders and expressed the view that "more people go to prison (and go to prison for longer periods) than they would if the option of the suspended sentence was not available". A power to suspend youth custody sentences was also opposed in comments on the Green Paper by the British Association of Social Workers, NACRO, the National Association of Probation Officers and the Conference of Chief Probation Officers, which suggested that "to a marked degree the young offender is less likely than the adult to go through the rational thought processes before becoming involved in further crime which are necessary for suspended sentences to be effective."

258 On the other hand, the Magistrates' Association stated in its comments on the Green Paper that, if the suspended sentence is available in respect of adults, it should also be available to young adults. It nevertheless hoped that such a power "would only be used in exceptional circumstances since this group of offenders is unlikely to be temperamentally suited to benefit from this type of sentence." Since the publication of the White Paper, however, the Association has decided not to press for a power to suspend a youth custody sentence. The Howard League for Penal Reform, while not convinced that the suspended sentence has proved a successful innovation, expressed the view that, while suspended sentences are on the statute book, they should be imposed on young adults in the same way as on adults.

259. In view of the lack of evidence that suspended sentences of imprisonment have reduced the prison population significantly if at all, we consider that the introduction of statutory criteria for custodial sentences, the shortening of sentences and the development of non-custodial alternatives are preferable and less hazardous approaches to reducing the numbers in custody. **We recommend that, when the youth custody sentence is introduced, there should be no provision for the suspension of a youth custody sentence.**

Supervision on release
260. Borstal and detention centre trainees and young prisoners who are not granted parole are subject on discharge to a period of supervision on licence. In the case of young offenders released from detention centres and borstals and young prisoners who have served sentences of less than 18 months, the supervision period is twelve months. Those serving sentences of 18 months or more are subject to supervision up to the end of the sentence.

261. The National Association of Probation Officers argues that, even if the court has taken care to explain to an offender at the time of sentence that a period in custody will be followed by a lengthy period on licence, many offenders feel that being faced with this length of licence is grossly unfair and amounts to being punished twice over. Many feel very resentful and, where this occurs, the length of licence may act as an impediment to the resettlement of the offender. We agree with the Association's view that it is difficult to justify lengthy terms of supervision after a short sentence in terms of justice, need for social work support or protection of the public.

262. Furthermore, in its evidence to us, the Association suggested that magistrates in particular regard offences committed on licence as being manifestations of an inability to respond to help offered under the auspices of a court order; yet there is a clear distinction between a negotiated contract to co-operate with a probation officer as an alternative to custody and an enforced extension of a custodial sentence. The Association argues that failure to perceive the difference "makes it extremely difficult to argue for many non-custodial alternatives for young offenders who return to court within a few months of release from DC's and borstals". It therefore concludes that "there may well come a time when the principle of statutory after-care for young offenders will have to be radically examined".

263. **We recommend that the long term aim should be to devote adequate resources to the through-care of young inmates, including regular visits to those serving youth custody sentences by probation officers and voluntary associates, so that all young offenders might be persuaded to take full advantage of voluntary after-care provision.** In the short term, we endorse the White Paper's proposal that liability to supervision after release should not greatly exceed the period in custody. It suggested that "shorter periods of supervision will enable supervising officers to focus their work in a more effective way" and that young adults should be subject to supervision on release for three months or until the date on which their full sentence would have expired, whichever is the longer, subject to a maximum of twelve months (para. 27).

264. This coincides with the view of the National Association of Probation Officers that, in the light of a greater emphasis on short term intensive work with probation clients, "it is clearly wasteful of scarce staff resources and unhelpful to the client to continue with unnecessarily long periods of supervision". Similarly, the Conference of Chief Probation Officers favours shorter, more focussed periods of licence supervision.

265. **We recommend that in the short term periods of compulsory supervision on release should be shortened, and young offenders should continue to be eligible for voluntary after-care from the probation and after-care service for up to a year after discharge.**

Recall

266. At present a young offender is liable to administrative recall at any time during the period of supervision for any breach of the requirements to which he is subject during supervision. In addition a young offender released under supervision from borstal training or from over 18 months in prison may be returned

to custody by the court if found guilty of an imprisonable offence while under supervision. The response to the previous Government's Green Paper revealed widespread support for the view that the decision to recall should be a judicial, not an administrative one, and that it is wrong to deprive a young person of his liberty without a court hearing.

267. The White Paper expressed support for this view and proposed that during the period of supervision a young offender should be liable to be brought before a magistrates' court for any breach of the conditions of supervision. When a breach is proved to the satisfaction of the court, it will be able to impose up to 30 days in custody or a fine not exceeding £200. If the offender commits a further offence during the supervision period, the court will be able to deal with the breach of supervision as just described in addition to any other sentence imposed for the further offence.

268. The view that decisions about recall should be taken by a court is supported by the Magistrates' Association, the Conference of Chief Probation Officers, the National Association of Probation Officers, the Howard League for Penal Reform, the British Association of Social Workers and the National Youth Bureau. In its comments on the Green Paper, the Conference of Chief Probation Officers argued that this would give the offender "a right of audience, the element of judicial impartiality and the value of recall being considered by the body which was involved in the initial custodial decision."

269. **We recommend that the decision to recall a young offender to a penal establishment should be made by a court.**

Detention centres
270. The original intention of detention centres, which were introduced by the Criminal Justice Act 1948, was that they should be primarily punitive and deterrent rather than reformative, and from the earliest discussions they acquired the label of being a "short sharp shock" treatment. However, from the outset detention centre staff found it difficult to sustain a solely negative approach to their charges. Four years after the opening of the first detention centre, the Annual Report of the Prison Commissioners made it clear that elements had been introduced which were intended to "elevate punishment into positive intensive training."

271. By the time of the report of the Advisory Council on the Penal System on "Detention Centres" (1970), detention in a detention centre had developed from being a special sentence designed for a limited category of offenders into the standard form of short term custodial sentence for young offenders in general. The Advisory Council recommended that "the punitive function of detention in a detention centre should be regarded as fulfilled by the deprivation of an offender's liberty". From this premise, it went on to recommend that positive training, particularly of an educational nature, should be formally incorporated in the approach of detention centres. The Advisory Council's recommendations were accepted in principle by the Government and resources were made available to fulfil the educational recommendations. Since then the detention centre has remained the standard short term sentence for young male offenders and in 1979 11,602 young men were received into detention centres, over 70 per

cent of whom had been convicted of theft and burglary offences.

272. Details of research comparing reconviction following different sentences (including non-custodial sentences) have been published in successive editions of the Home Office handbook for sentencers, "The Sentence of the Court". These indicate that, once the type of offender has been taken into account (i.e. in terms of age and number and type of previous convictions), reconviction rates for detention centres differ very little from other forms of sentence. The latest reconviction figures are for offenders discharged in 1976 and followed up for two years. The reconviction figure for those leaving junior detention centres is 75 per cent and for those leaving senior centres 57 per cent: the overall rate is 65 per cent.

273. A recent study by Margaret Norris, "Offenders in Residential Communities — Measuring and Understanding Change" (Howard Journal, Vol. 18, No. 1), compared change in matched samples of 199 residents of the Surrey Community Development Trust, a project providing residential accommodation for probation service clients, and 58 detention centre trainees. The study found that, by the end of their sentences, there was a significant increase in the number of detention centre trainees showing a tendency to become rebels and break rules as evidence of their ability to stand on their own two feet. A much higher proportion of a matched sample of Trust residents aspired to become less rule breaking and only 12 per cent ended up as "rebels", compared with 36 per cent of the detention centre trainees.

274. We are sceptical of the value of the detention centre sentence, except for relatively well adjusted young offenders from reasonably stable backgrounds. In particular, the young offender who has been used to an excessive degree of physical punishment or shouted discipline at home is only likely to have his attitudes reinforced by the detention centre regime.

275. At present the courts are advised to refrain from passing detention centre sentences on certain types of young offender. Home Office Circular No. 179/1972 drew the courts' attention to the demanding nature of the detention centre regime and stated:

"To obtain any benefit from detention, offenders must be fit for the regime and any with severe physical disability or overt mental disorder should be excluded".

The severity of a disability is to be judged by its likelihood to interrupt training. However, the circular states that centres can accept those with minor conditions which can be dealt with in the centre including "well controlled diabetics and epileptics, or those with minor fractures which are well on the way to full union". Since there are no facilities for psychiatric treatment at detention centres, cases of mental illness are not acceptable.

276. Nevertheless, the available evidence suggests that many of those entering detention centres are far from stable young men. The Winter 1978 edition of the "Prison Medical Journal" contained an article entitled "The Health of Detention Centre Boys" by Charles Backhouse, medical officer at Send detention centre, which analysed the medical histories of trainees at that establishment. In

addition to discovering a higher incidence than expected of physical disease, Dr. Backhouse found that:

"A history of depression, suicidal gestures, and overdoses is common, the latter particularly so in the small group giving a history of drug abuse."

The latter group constituted 11-12 per cent of Send trainees. Anxiety and depression, serious enough to require special observation and drug treatment, was found in about 5 per cent of boys. Dr Backhouse concluded that "the mental health of these young boys would be improved by more education, and more stimulating occupations."

277. In April 1980 new experimental tougher regimes began operating at two centres, New Hall senior detention centre and Send, a junior centre. The new regimes include increased emphasis on a more sustained pace in carrying out tasks, more physical education, fewer privileges, less association, an earlier time for lights out and an increase in the number of parades, inspections and drill sessions. At Send the staff now wear uniform and at New Hall the Construction Industry Training Course, which involved boys in practical work experience and training intended to fit them for employment on release, has been closed on the ground that it is inappropriate to a tougher regime. On 23 March 1981, the Home Secretary announced that similar regimes would be introduced at Haslar senior detention centre and Foston junior detention centre.

278. The Government has stressed the experimental nature of this development and has acknowledged that there are no research findings which suggest that tougher regimes will produce lower reconviction rates than more constructive ones: indeed, studies throughout the prison, borstal and community home systems have found little difference in reconviction rates as a result of different styles of regime. There has been little research into the effects of variations in detention centre regimes as such, although a study was carried out on senior detention centre trainees who were at Latchmere House (then a detention centre) from 1969 until early 1971. In a letter to Mr. Mark Carlisle Q.C., M.P., of 15 August 1978, Lord Harris, then Minister of State, stated:

"There were a number of staff changes during the period in question which made it difficult to assess the effects of the differing regimes, but it did appear that in the case of three months' sentences there was no difference in the reconviction rate resulting from the three different types of regime."

279. Like the Advisory Council on the Penal System, we consider that the punitive function of detention in a detention centre should be regarded as fulfilled by the deprivation of liberty, and we therefore deplore the philosophy behind the introduction of the experimental tougher regimes. **We recommend that detention centre regimes should be as constructive as possible within the limitations of the short period in custody.**

280. In recent years, the Magistrates' Association has consistently argued that courts should be enabled to impose detention centre sentences of less than three months. The White Paper accordingly proposed that the minimum and maxi-

mum periods of detention should be reduced to three weeks and four months respectively, and stated:

> "This is because the deterrent effect of a sentence of this kind is likely to diminish after the first few weeks and because the courts should have the opportunity, when they believe that a custodial sentence is unavoidable, to make it as short as possible" (para. 15).

281. The Justices' Clerks' Society proposed even shorter sentences in its paper, "Child Law Reform", suggesting that a sentence as short as five days in a detention centre would be quite feasible. The Society argued that in those five days the young offender "would still be extremely unhappy at being there and would not have recovered his pride in being able to 'do his time' ". The Prison and Borstal Governors' Branch of the Society of Civil and Public Servants also advocated a five days minimum sentence in its comments on the Green Paper. The Expenditure Committee recommended in its report of 1975 that courts should be enabled to impose detention centre sentences of between two days and three weeks in addition to longer sentences.

282. While there is general support for the proposition that custodial sentences should in general be shorter, several organisations have expressed concern that the courts are likely to impose the new short detention centre sentences on many young offenders who would now be given a non-custodial sentence. This would be contrary to the intentions of the Magistrates' Association which, in advocating shorter sentences, has consistently argued that these should be imposed instead of longer ones and not instead of non-custodial sentences. Nevertheless, the Conference of Chief Probation Officers suggested in its comments in the White Paper that its proposals "will lead to significantly larger numbers of young offenders being sentenced to custody, and at earlier stages in their criminal careers, than is the case at present."

283. Observing that the proposals "involve using what is and must always be the measure of last resort at early stages", the Conference continued:

> "The proposals if implemented could create a situation where, in a generation's time, a significant proportion of the population, particularly the male population of certain groups of society, will have had an experience of custody in their early years; an outcome to be viewed, on any reckoning, with serious concern."

It pointed out that the deterrent effects of short periods in custody are unproven and that there are other well established ways of keeping suitably selected offenders from committing further crime for reasonable periods of time. The Conference recommended retaining three months as the minimum sentence for juveniles in the hope of ensuring that this measure remains high on the sentencing tariff.

284. Similar fears were voiced by the Association of Community Homes, the Association of Directors of Social Services, the Association of Metropolitan Authorities, the British Association of Social Workers, NACRO, the National Association of Probation Officers, the National Council for Voluntary Organisations, the National Youth Bureau and New Approaches to Juvenile Crime in

their comments on the White Paper. The ADSS suggested that the change will also lead in the long run to more people progressing to youth custody and prison since, when a young person who has been in a detention centre for three weeks subsequently offends again, the court will see little alternative to a youth custody order.

285. While we are persuaded that the case for shorter maximum and minimum detention centre sentences is overwhelming, the implementation of the White Paper's proposals as they stand would almost certainly result in a large increase in the number of young offenders receiving custodial sentences. **We recommend that the maximum and minimum periods of detention in a detention centre should be reduced, but this should be combined with safeguards to prevent the new shorter sentences from being used where non-custodial sentences would now be imposed. Our proposal for legislative criteria stipulating the circumstances in which youth custody sentences may be imposed should apply also to detention centre sentences.**

Juveniles in custody
286. On 30 June 1980 there were 2,039 juveniles in prison department establishments in England and Wales. 932 were in borstals, 756 in detention centres, 299 in remand centres and 52 in adult prisons.

287. The first category of juveniles in custody is the defendants under 17 years old who are remanded or committed to adult prisons and remand centres to await trial or sentence, who numbered 301 on 30 June 1980. In 1979, 3,671 juveniles were remanded or committed in prison department custody. More than a quarter of those so remanded are subsequently acquitted or receive non-custodial sentences.

288. Courts are empowered to remand juveniles in custody by Section 23 of the Children and Young Persons Act 1969. This stipulates that when a court remands or commits a juvenile, if it certifies that he is of so unruly a character that he cannot safely be committed to the care of the local authority, it shall commit him to a remand centre or, if no remand centre is available, to a prison. In addition to remands under unruly certificates, Section 28 of the Magistrates' Courts Act 1952 provides that a convicted young person for whom a borstal sentence is recommended by a juvenile court must either be released on bail or committed to a prison department establishment pending his appearance in the Crown Court for sentence.

289. The Expenditure Committee said in its report of 1975:

> "We condemn in the strongest possible terms the use of certificates of unruliness as a means of achieving secure accommodation. We recommend that the practice of remanding young persons to adult prisons should cease forthwith; alternative arrangements must be made" (para. 23).

290. It is now universally agreed that such custodial remands are undesirable and that, where a remand to secure conditions is necessary, this should ideally be to a secure unit in a local authority establishment staffed by those specialising in work with children, rather than to a prison department establishment. Section 71 of the Children's Act 1975 enables financial provision to be made for such

units by way of grants to local authorities from central government, and grants to local authorities for the provision of secure accommodation between 1976/77 and 1980/81 exceeded £6 million.

291. In 1977 the Certificate of Unruly Character (Conditions) Order restricted the circumstances in which remanding juveniles in custody is permissible. This is now only possible if the young person is charged with an offence punishable in the case of an adult with imprisonment of 14 years or more, is charged with an offence of violence or has been found guilty on a previous occasion of a violent offence, or has persistently absconded from or seriously disrupted the running of a community home. In addition the court has to be satisfied on the basis of a written report from the local authority that no suitable accommodation is available for the young person in a community home unless, in the case of the first two categories, the court is remanding the young person for the first time in the proceedings and is satisfied that there has not been time to obtain such a report.

292. The coming into operation of the Order on 1st August 1977 was followed immediately by a sharp drop in the number of young people remanded in custody, in contrast with a steady rise in numbers earlier in the year. As a result of this Order, and a series of Orders which have ended the issuing of unruly certificates for juvenile girls, the number of juveniles remanded or committed in custody fell from 4,812 in 1976 to 3,671 in 1979. It is noteworthy that a reduction in the number of remands in custody did not automatically follow an increase in local authority secure places — the number of such places had been increasing for several years, as had the number of juveniles remanded in custody — but only occured when the courts' powers to make custodial remands were restricted.

293. The White Paper announced that the remand of 14 year old boys to prison department establishments, of whom there were about 360 in 1979, would be brought to an end in March 1981. Custodial remands of 15 and 16 year old boys are to continue for the present, but the Government has affirmed its intention to phase out such remands when resources allow this.

294. We recommend that a specific timetable should be announced for ending the remand of 15 and 16 year olds to prison department establishments and rapid progress should be made towards this objective.

295. The second category of juveniles in custody consists of those who have received sentences of borstal training or of detention in a detention centre. The 1969 Children and Young Persons Act provided for the phasing out of the sentences of borstal training and detention in a detention centre for those under 17. Despite the Act's intentions, the number of juveniles committed to borstal rose from 818 in 1969 to 1,683 in 1979 and the number sent to detention centres increased from 2,228 in 1969 to 5,478 in 1979 — a very much faster increase than the rise in juvenile crime over the period. The proportion of boys aged 14-16 found guilty of indictable or triable-either-way offences who were given custodial sentences rose from 6 per cent in 1969 to 12 per cent in 1979. As Mr Leon Brittan Q.C., M.P., pointed out in a speech in Derby on 16th November 1979:

"During the past twenty years, the proportion of convicted adults received into custody has been more than halved. During the same period the proportion of juveniles receiving custodial sentences . . . has more than tripled. In 1955 an adult was 20 times more likely than a juvenile to get a custodial sentence for an indictable offence. Now he is only twice as likely."

296. The ineffectiveness of prison department custody for this age group is illustrated by the fact that 75 per cent of the juveniles leaving detention centres and 84 per cent of those leaving borstals in 1976 (the latest year for which figures are available) were convicted of further offences within the next two years.

297. A substantial number of juveniles are sent to penal institutions with no previous attempt to deal with their delinquent behaviour by supervision in the community. A recent Home Office study found that just over a third of the juveniles entering borstal in 1977 had not previously been subject to a supervision order. The figure for detention centres appeared even higher: of 130 junior detention centre trainees from the Prison Department South West region and adjoining counties in November 1977, 78 per cent had not previously been under supervision. More recently, a Parliamentary answer of 25 January 1980 revealed that, of boys received into Send detention centre between 1 October and 31 December 1978, 40 per cent had had a previous supervision order. In 1979, 16 per cent of the juveniles received into detention centres had no previous convictions and 43 per cent had one or two previous convictions.

298. We consider that, before a custodial sentence is imposed on a juvenile, all possible alternatives should have been considered. Our proposed legislative criteria for the imposition of custodial sentences should help to ensure this. In addition, **we recommend that recommendations for custodial sentences for juveniles in social enquiry reports should be discussed with a senior staff member in the probation service or social services department preparing the report, with a view to ensuring that all alternatives have been thoroughly explored. We further recommend that, when a recommendation for a custodial sentence is contained in a report by a social worker or probation officer, or where no specific recommendation is made and custody is envisaged, the court should ask the social services or the probation service what alternatives have been considered.**

299. The 1969 Act's aim of ending custodial sentences for this age group has the support of prison and borstal governors. In its comments on the Green Paper, the Governors' Branch of the Society of Civil and Public Servants, while accepting that junior detention centres would continue to be used for juveniles in the immediate future, added:

"We strongly believe that this approach should be regarded as what it is, a temporary expediency forced on us by the lack of positive action by the social services. This view needs to be reinforced by stipulating a specific date by which the junior detention centre sentence is brought to an end."

300. In contrast, the White Paper proposed that the new youth custody

sentence will apply to 15 and 16 year olds with a maximum period of 12 months, and that in addition boys of 14 and over will continue to be eligible for detention centre sentences. These changes reflect "the Government's firm commitment to custodial provision for a minority of juveniles" (para. 46). The Government accordingly proposes to repeal the provisions of the Children and Young Persons Act 1969 under which detention of the under seventeens in detention centres was to be phased out.

301. In its comments on the White Paper, New Approaches to Juvenile Crime regretted the Government's commitment to perpetuate the use of prison department establishments in new legislation over a decade after legislation which envisaged the phasing out of penal custody for the under seventeens. New Approaches acknowledged that

> "There are of course some young people who pose so serious a threat to society and to themselves that they must be placed in secure accommodation, but this represents only a small proportion of juvenile offenders and the secure accommodation required to contain them should (given present legislation) ideally be provided by the DHSS and local authorities rather than by the Prison Department."

Similarly, the Conference of Chief Probation Officers in its comments on the White Paper expressed opposition to the continuation of detention centres for juvenile offenders. The Association of Directors of Social Services described the proposal to repeal Section 7 (3) of the 1969 Act as "a matter of great regret", the British Association of Social Workers reasserted its opposition to the continued use of borstals and detention centres for juveniles and the Residential Care Association stated that it viewed with concern the continued use of penal establishments for juveniles. The National Association of Probation Officers also argued that "penal custody is inappropriate for juvenile offenders".

302. In Chapter IV above we drew attention to the Government's acceptance of the recommendation of the Black Committee on legislation and services for children and young persons in Northern Ireland that all existing custodial and residential sentences for juvenile offenders should be amalgamated into a single determinate residential order. We consider the arguments for this approach to be as valid in the case of England and Wales as in Northern Ireland.

303. **We recommend that the Government should announce a timetable for a progressive raising of the minimum age for entering youth custody centres or detention centres until the minimum age for both is 17.**

304. The third and most problematic category of juveniles in custody comprises those sentenced under Section 53 of the Children and Young Persons Act 1933. This provides that, where a person under 18 is convicted of murder he will be sentenced to be detained "during Her Majesty's pleasure." Further, if a juvenile is convicted on indictment of an offence for which an adult could receive 14 years' imprisonment or more (e.g. manslaughter, robbery or burglary) the court may, if no other method is suitable, sentence the offender to be detained in such place and on such conditions as the Secretary of State may direct.

305. In 1979, 80 young men and women were sentenced under Section 53 — a 60 per cent increase on the 1973 figure of 50 and a more than six-fold increase on the 1971 figure of 12. During 1979 a further two young men sentenced under similar legislation in Scotland were received on transfer. 8 of the 82 offenders were allocated to community homes, 3 to a youth treatment centre, 33 to borstals and 38 to young prisoner centres. On 31 October 1980, 27 juveniles sentenced under Section 53 were detained in prison department establishments, 24 in community homes and 11 in youth treatment centres.

306. In 1979 the Magistrates' Association at its Annual General Meeting adopted a resolution expressing concern at the lack of facilities for accommodating young persons detained under Section 53 and urging the Government "to take urgent steps to remedy the situation." The Prison Officers' Association also expressed concern about this group of young people in its comments on the Advisory Council on the Penal System's report, "Young Adult Offenders", and proposed that joint consultation be undertaken to determine the validity of accommodating them in young offender establishments. **We recommend that the Government should take urgent steps to ensure that all juveniles detained under Section 53 of the Children and Young Persons Act 1933 are accommodated in establishments suited to the needs of disturbed juveniles, rather than in prison department establishments.**

Summary of recommendations

1. Borstal training and imprisonment for young adults should be combined into a single determinate sentence of youth custody (para. 222).

2. Placing offenders in establishments near their homes should receive a high priority in decisions concerning the allocation of offenders between youth custody centres (para. 225).

3. Those offenders for whom a custodial sentence exceeding four months is inappropriate but who are mentally unfit for detention centre regimes should not receive any form of custodial sentence (para. 227).

4. When custodial sentences are imposed on mentally ill or disordered young offenders, the Prison Department should ensure that these are served in establishments or units which are geared as far as possible to the special needs of such offenders (para. 228).

5. Governors of establishments containing young people sentenced to youth custody should be empowered to apply to a court of the same status as the original sentencing court for variation of a youth custody sentence (para. 229).

6. Young adult women in custody should be located in small youth custody units attached to male establishments, and opportunities should be developed for co-educational activities involving both male and female young offenders in custody (para. 235).

7. Suitable training regimes should be provided for all those sentenced to youth custody. These should incorporate facilities of a high standard for

work, vocational training, education and the development of social skills (para. 240).

8. Training for those sentenced to youth custody should be provided in conjunction with facilities in the community, and there should be more day release to outside education and training facilities (para. 242).

9. Every encouragement should be given to young offenders to continue courses begun in youth custody centres after discharge (para. 242).

10. Legislation should provide that a youth custody sentence should be imposed only when the offender is a real danger to society or has shown himself unwilling or unable to respond to non-custodial penalties. A court on passing a youth custody sentence should give its reasons for this conclusion, and this part of the process should form grounds for appeal (para. 250).

11. Time spent in custody on remand should count towards a youth custody sentence (para. 253).

12. The courts should be asked to consider time spent on remand in local authority establishments when considering the length of a custodial sentence (para. 253).

13. When the youth custody sentence is introduced, there should be no provision for the suspension of a youth custody sentence (para. 259).

14. The long term aim should be to devote adequate resources to the through-care of young inmates, including regular visits to those serving youth custody sentences by probation officers and voluntary associates, so that all young offenders might be persuaded to take full advantage of voluntary after-care provision (para. 263).

15. In the short term periods of compulsory supervision on release should be shortened, and young offenders should continue to be eligible for voluntary after-care from the probation and after-care service for up to a year after discharge (para. 265).

16. The decision to recall a young offender to a penal establishment should be made by a court (para. 269).

17. Detention centre regimes should be as constructive as possible within the limitations of the short period in custody (para. 279).

18. The maximum and minimum periods of detention in a detention centre should be reduced, but this should be combined with safeguards to prevent the new shorter sentences from being used where non-custodial sentences would now be imposed. Our proposal for legislative criteria stipulating the circumstances in which youth custody sentences may be imposed should apply also to detention centre sentences (para. 285).

19. A specific timetable should be announced for ending the remand of 15 and 16 year olds to prison department establishments and rapid progress should be made towards this objective (para. 294).

20. Recommendations for custodial sentences for juveniles in social enquiry

reports should be discussed with a senior staff member in the probation service or social services department preparing the report, with a view to ensuring that all alternatives have been thoroughly explored (para. 298).

21. When a recommendation for a custodial sentence is contained in a report by a social worker or a probation officer or where no specific recommendation is made and custody is envisaged, the court should ask the social services or the probation service what alternatives have been considered (para. 298).

22. The Government should announce a timetable for a progressive raising of the minimum age for entering youth custody centres or detention centres until the minimum age for both is 17 (para. 303).

23. The Government should take urgent steps to ensure that all juveniles detained under Section 53 of the Children and Young Persons Act 1933 are accommodated in establishments suited to the needs of disturbed juveniles, rather than in prison department establishments (para. 306).

307. Although we have found some genuine difference of view on important matters of detail, we have also discovered an encouraging measure of agreement over many broad issues of policy and practice concerning young offenders among most of the organisations and individuals from whom we have received evidence, and this is reflected in our recommendations.

308. Our proposals are designed to ensure that the trend towards the increasing institutionalisation of juvenile offenders is reversed and that an increasing proportion of both juvenile and young adult offenders are dealt with in the community; that the system of police cautioning is supported, extended and made more consistent; that a comprehensive range of alternatives to custody, including intermediate treatment programmes, professional fostering schemes, community service schemes, attendance centres and probation "packages", is developed and used in all areas of the country; that the courts' confidence in supervision in the community is increased; that the courts are equipped to deal more appropriately with the minority of young offenders who require an element of punishment and secure containment; and that, for the minority of young offenders who continue to experience them, custodial regimes are as constructive as possible and geared to the offender's reintegration into the community.

309. In these objectives we believe that we are at one with the reports of the Expenditure Committee and the Advisory Council on the Penal System, with the majority of professional and other informed opinion and with the stated aims of the present Government. Above all, we believe that our proposals would result in a more humane, more cost effective and more just response to offending by juveniles and young adults and a more rational framework for attempting to contain crime among the young.

SUMMARY OF RECOMMENDATIONS

Diversion from the criminal justice system
1. The use of the caution should be sanctioned in legislation and attention should be given to achieving greater consistency in cautioning practice throughout the country (para. 25).

2. All first-time minor offenders under seventeen who admit guilt should be cautioned, and this should also be the normal practice in regard to those who commit a second minor offence (para. 26).

3. Formal cautions should not be administered where there is insufficient evidence for prosecution (para. 29).

4. Cautioning should be used more often for young adult offenders (para. 30).

5. The function of prosecution should be performed by a service independent of the service responsible for the investigation of offences (para. 34).

Community-based provision for young offenders

6. Professional fostering schemes should be supported and extended and the DHSS should give local authorities positive guidance and encouragement to develop such schemes (para. 51).

7. There should be a range of intermediate treatment, catering both for young offenders and those at risk. Within this range, greater efforts should be made to provide intermediate treatment for juveniles who would otherwise have been committed to custodial and residential establishments (para. 61).

8. Before imposing an intermediate treatment requirement, the court should satisfy itself that the programme envisaged by the social worker or probation officer is appropriate (para. 67).

9. Intermediate treatment requirements should be mandatory and their implementation should not be left to the supervisor's discretion. However, discretion should be given to the supervising officer to modify the detailed content of the intermediate treatment programme in the light of changing circumstances (para. 67).

10. Local authorities should be encouraged to transfer resources from residential care to intermediate treatment. This transfer should be achieved in a manner which ensures that the resulting smaller scale residential sector is adequately financed with a complement of well trained and highly valued staff (para. 68).

11. The extra finance intended for the development of intermediate treatment which is to be added to the rate support grant should be increased to a level at least comparable with the extra £5 million necessitated by the proposed residential care order. This should be combined with a statutory requirement on local authorities to provide certain minimum levels of intermediate treatment (para. 69).

12. The probation service should be enabled to provide intermediate treatment facilities in a way which is consistent with proper co-ordination of local arrangements (para. 73).

13. There should be increased central government funding for intermediate treatment schemes run by voluntary organisations, and in particular there should be a considerable further increase in the funds available to the Rainer Foundation Intermediate Treatment Fund (para. 77).

14. Greater encouragement and support for voluntary initiatives in intermediate treatment should be provided by the statutory services (para. 77).

15. Consideration should be given to the establishment of an appropriate system of joint financing for the development of intermediate treatment (para. 79).

16. The provision of the Children and Young Persons Act 1969 for the phasing out of attendance centres should be repealed. The number of junior and senior attendance centres should be increased until both types of centre are available to courts in at least all the main centres of population for offenders of both sexes (para. 86).

17. Links should be developed between attendance centres and intermediate treatment schemes, so that young offenders wishing to continue participation in constructive activities after the expiry of the attendance order can be channelled into voluntary participation in intermediate treatment (para. 86).

18. Careful research should accompany the extension of attendance centres, to monitor the extent to which they are used for offenders who would otherwise receive custodial sentences (para. 86).

19. There should be a greater use of the fine for young adult offenders (para. 87).

20. A fine should not be imposed on the parents of a juvenile offender unless there is clear evidence that parental responsibilities have been neglected (para. 91).

21. Legislation concerning the imposition of fines on the parents of juvenile offenders should specify factors which the courts should take into account in deciding whether this course would be unreasonable in the particular case (para. 93).

22. Social enquiry reports should comment more substantially than at present on the implications of possible court decisions involving the responsibility of parents (para. 93).

23. There should be a continuing extension of community service orders (para. 99).

24. Community service orders should be available for 16 year olds, and the probation service should receive adequate additional resources in recognition of the careful selection and close supervision required for this age group (para. 99).

25. Forms of community service for juvenile offenders should be developed within intermediate treatment programmes and should be used in particular as an alternative to custodial and residential disposals (para. 105).

26. Schemes involving selected young adult offenders in full time training based on work in social services settings, in combination with a probation order and with a view to obtaining full time employment in due course, should be more widely developed (para. 109).

27. Schemes providing community service placements for difficult and delinquent young people in care should be further developed (para. 115).

28. Restitution schemes for young offenders should be established on an experimental basis in a few areas. These experiments should be carefully monitored and the results used as a basis for assessing whether this approach should be developed more widely (para. 121).

29. The Home Secretary should issue guidance encouraging the further development of probation "packages", whereby a clearly stated programme of activities and methods of intervention is spelled out to the court in a social enquiry report (para. 144).

30. There should be a greatly increased provision for those under 21 of hostels and other forms of accommodation, day centres, educational and employment schemes, and facilities for drug dependents and problem drinkers. Where there are conflicting demands on resources, priority should be given to facilities for this age group (para. 144).

31. A permanent system of central government funding for facilities for problem drinkers and drug misusers should be established (para. 145).

32. Each probation area should identify the gaps in provision for young adult offenders and, in co-operation with social services departments and other relevant agencies, should develop a strategy to fill those gaps (para. 146).

33. In all local authority areas arrangements should be made for regular consultation between those agencies which are concerned with young offenders and young people at risk (para. 150).

34. Those children's regional planning committees which have not yet done so should co-opt magistrates (para. 153).

35. There should be a thorough evaluation and monitoring of systems of co-ordination in several areas of the country with a view to producing guidelines for good practice which would be of national application. In the light of the results of this evaluation, the Government should consider whether a statutory duty should be imposed on local authorities to establish inter-agency committees to discuss and co-ordinate policies concerning juvenile delinquency (para. 156).

36. Arrangements for the inter-change of staff between agencies concerned with young offenders and young people at risk should be encouraged and developed more widely (para. 158).

37. More social workers should be encouraged to specialise in work with juveniles and those working with this age group should receive appropriate specialised training, including training in court procedure (para. 161).

Care orders and the use of residential care for young offenders
38. Care orders should no longer be an available option in criminal proceedings, but should be replaced by a new determinate residential order designed for a small minority of persistent or serious young offenders who require an element of punishment (represented by loss of liberty, not by a harsh or negative regime) and secure containment (para. 187).

39. In the short term:
(i) An offer of legal representation for the child and his or her parents should be mandatory before a care order is made (para. 191).
(ii) The position of a young offender subject to a care order should be regularly reviewed by a body including one or more members of the

juvenile bench before which the child, his parents and foster parents where appropriate should have the right to appear (para. 194).

(iii) More precise criteria for the making of care orders in criminal proceedings should be laid down by statute or by guidance to courts and local authorities (para. 196).

(iv) When a recommendation for a care order is contained in a report by a social worker or probation officer, the court should ask the social services or probation service what alternatives have been considered (para. 196).

40. There should be a shift of emphasis and resources from residential observation and assessment towards non-residential assessment, including observation and assessment in the family home wherever possible. Better use should be made of child guidance clinics for the assessment of children who need not be removed from home (para. 205).

41. In appropriate cases an assessment period should be used as an opportunity for positive assistance to the child and the family (para. 205).

42. Criteria for the use of secure accommodation should be incorporated in statutory regulations (para. 214).

43. Any decision by a three-monthly review committee to continue the detention of a young person in secure accommodation should be subject to confirmation by the juvenile court. An offer of legal representation for the child at the court hearing should be mandatory (para. 214).

Custodial measures

44. Borstal training and imprisonment for young adults should be combined into a single determinate sentence of youth custody (para. 222).

45. Placing offenders in establishments near their homes should receive a high priority in decisions concerning the allocation of offenders between youth custody centres (para. 225).

46. Those offenders for whom a custodial sentence exceeding four months is inappropriate but who are mentally unfit for detention centre regimes should not receive any form of custodial sentence (para. 227).

47. When custodial sentences are imposed on mentally ill or disordered young offenders, the Prison Department should ensure that these are served in establishments or units which are geared as far as possible to the special needs of such offenders (para. 228).

48. Governors of establishments containing young people sentenced to youth custody should be empowered to apply to a court of the same status as the original sentencing court for variation of a youth custody sentence (para. 229).

49. Young adult women in custody should be located in small youth custody units attached to male establishments, and opportunities should be developed for co-educational activities involving both male and female young offenders in custody (para. 235).

50. Suitable training regimes should be provided for all those sentenced to

youth custody. These should incorporate facilities of a high standard for work, vocational training, education and the development of social skills (para. 240).

51. Training for those sentenced to youth custody should be provided in conjunction with facilities in the community, and there should be more day release to outside education and training facilities (para. 242).

52. Every encouragement should be given to young offenders to continue courses begun in youth custody after discharge (para. 242).

53. Legislation should provide that a youth custody sentence should be imposed only when the offender is a real danger to society or has shown himself unwilling or unable to respond to non-custodial penalties. A court on passing a youth custody sentence should give its reasons for this conclusion, and this part of the process should form grounds for appeal (para. 250).

54. Time spent in custody on remand should count towards a youth custody sentence (para. 253).

55. The courts should be asked to consider time spent on remand in local authority establishments when considering the length of a custodial sentence (para. 253).

56. When the youth custody sentence is introduced, there should be no provision for the suspension of a youth custody sentence (para. 259).

57. The long term aim should be to devote adequate resources to the through-care of young inmates, including regular visits to those serving youth custody sentences by probation officers and voluntary associates, so that all young offenders might be persuaded to take full advantage of voluntary after-care provision (para. 263).

58. In the short term periods of compulsory supervision on release should be shortened, and young offenders should continue to be eligible for voluntary after-care from the probation and after-care service for up to a year after discharge (para. 265).

59. The decision to recall a young offender to a penal establishment should be made by a court (para. 269).

60. Detention centre regimes should be as constructive as possible within the limitations of the short period in custody (para. 279).

61. The maximum and minimum periods of detention in a detention centre should be reduced, but this should be combined with safeguards to prevent the new shorter sentences from being used where non-custodial sentences would now be imposed. Our proposal for legislative criteria stipulating the circumstances in which youth custody sentences may be imposed should apply also to detention centre sentences (para. 285).

62. A specific timetable should be announced for ending the remand of 15 and 16 year olds to prison department establishments and rapid progress should be made towards this objective (para. 294).

63. Recommendations for custodial sentences for juveniles in social enquiry reports should be discussed with a senior staff member in the probation service or social services department preparing the report, with a view to ensuring that all alternatives have been thoroughly explored (para. 298).

64. When a recommendation for a custodial sentence is contained in a report by a social worker or a probation officer, or where no specific recommendation is made and custody is envisaged, the court should ask the social services or the probation service what alternatives have been considered (para. 298).

65. The Government should announce a timetable for a progressive raising of the minimum age for entering youth custody centres or detention centres until the minimum age for both is 17 (para. 303).

66. The Government should take urgent steps to ensure that all juveniles detained under Section 53 of the Children and Young Persons Act 1933 are accommodated in establishments suited to the needs of disturbed juveniles, rather than in prison department establishments (para. 306).

APPENDIX I: TRENDS IN JUVENILE AND YOUNG ADULT CRIME

Offenders found guilty of, or cautioned for, indictable/triable-either-way offences per 100,000 population in the age group by sex and age

England and Wales — Number of offenders per 100,000 population

Year	Males				Females			
	All ages	Aged 10 and under 14	Aged 14 and under 17	Aged 17 and under 21	All ages	Aged 10 and under 14	Aged 14 and under 17	Aged 17 and under 21
Indictable offences								
1959	926	2,317	3,224	2,713	105	213	336	230
1960	984	2,501	3,455	2,911	117	259	373	267
1961	1,061	2,816	3,544	2,996	137	323	416	294
1962	1,152	2,883	3,636	3,187	158	345	448	303
1963	1,227	2,837	3,986	3,472	160	342	457	309
1964	1,207	2,763	4,249	3,366	170	367	571	315
1965	1,262	2,741	4,481	3,594	184	397	683	333
1966	1,331	2,717	4,611	3,859	188	393	743	361
1967	1,357	2,715	4,602	3,898	196	396	665	387
1968	1,454	2,809	5,060	4,503	207	410	720	428
1969	1,615	3,013	5,709	5,245	238	471	824	516
1970	1,726	3,123	6,233	5,673	262	533	932	593
1971	1,790	3,235	6,561	5,854	293	605	1,125	670
1972	1,816	3,366	6,871	5,795	315	736	1,189	692
1973	1,816	3,411	7,072	5,810	310	775	1,209	687
1974	2,001	3,809	8,191	6,215	367	922	1,490	796
1975	2,075	3,522	7,861	6,689	398	894	1,514	889
1976	2,086	3,303	7,567	6,567	415	819	1,468	887
1977	2,182	3,792	7,995	6,654	451	1,058	1,610	942
1978	2,125	3,442	7,858	6,685	434	987	1,617	925
Indictable/triable-either-way offences								
1977	2,147	3,517	7,517	6,273	448	1,041	1,570	940
1978	2,074	3,187	7,382	6,245	430	952	1,572	915
1979	2,032	2,923	6,810	6,234	410	913	1,457	925

APPENDIX II: TRENDS IN SENTENCING

Percentage of persons aged 10 and under 14 sentenced for indictable/triable-either-way offences who received various sentences by sex and type of sentence or order

England and Wales

Percentage of total persons sentenced

Sex and year	Total	Conditional discharge	Probation or supervision order	Fine	Attendance centre order	Care order (fit person order or approved school)	Otherwise dealt with
Males				Indictable offences			
1969	100	28	29	19	11	9	4
1970	100	28	27	20	12	10	3
1971	100	26	28	20	12	12	3
1972	100	27	26	20	13	12	3
1973	100	26	25	22	12	12	2
1974	100	29	24	22	12	12	2
1975	100	30	23	21	13	12	2
1976	100	31	21	21	14	11	1
1977	100	32	21	22	13	9	2
1978	100	32	20	23	14	9	2
			Indictable/triable-either-way offences				
1977	100	31	22	22	14	10	1
1978	100	31	21	23	14	10	1
1979	100	29	22	22	17	9	1
Females				Indictable offences			
1969	100	35	33	21	*	7	4
1970	100	34	30	26	*	8	3
1971	100	32	31	24	*	10	3
1972	100	30	35	23	*	10	3
1973	100	30	30	26	*	11	3
1974	100	33	32	22	*	11	2
1975	100	34	30	21	*	12	2
1976	100	39	27	24	*	9	2
1977	100	37	26	25	*	10	2
1978	100	36	25	28	*	10	1
			Indictable/triable-either-way offences				
1977	100	37	27	25	*	10	2
1978	100	35	26	28	*	10	1
1979	100	35	26	30	—(¹)	8	1

* Not applicable   —(¹) Less than ½ per cent.

Percentage of persons aged 14 and under 17 sentenced for indictable/triable-either-way offences who received various sentences by sex and type of sentence or order

England and Wales

Percentage of total persons sentenced

Sex and year	Total	Conditional discharge	Probation or supervision order	Fine	Attendance centre order	Detention centre order	Care order (fit person order or approved school)	Borstal training	Otherwise dealt with
Males					*Indictable offences*				
1969	100	18	23	37	6	4	7	2	3
1970	100	17	22	38	7	4	8	2	2
1971	100	17	19	40	7	4	8	2	2
1972	100	17	17	42	7	5	7	3	2
1973	100	17	17	40	8	6	7	3	2
1974	100	18	17	40	9	6	6	3	2
1975	100	19	16	39	9	7	6	3	2
1976	100	20	15	38	9	8	5	3	2
1977	100	20	15	39	10	8	4	3	1
1978	100	19	14	40	11	9	4	3	1
					Indictable/triable-either-way offences				
1977	100	19	16	38	10	9	5	3	1
1978	100	18	14	39	11	9	4	3	1
1979	100	17	16	37	13	9	4	3	1
Females					*Indictable offences*				
1969	100	26	32	32	*	*	7	3	3
1970	100	26	30	34	*	*	8	(1)	3
1971	100	26	27	34	*	*	9	(1)	3
1972	100	24	26	37	*	*	10	1	3
1973	100	24	27	34	*	*	11	1	3
1974	100	26	26	36	*	*	1	9	2
1975	100	28	26	33	*	*	10	1	2
1976	100	29	23	35	*	*	9	1	2
1977	100	29	23	37	*	*	8	1	2
1978	100	29	22	40	*	*	7	1	1
					Indictable/triable-either-way offences				
1977	100	28	24	37	*	*	9	1	2
1978	100	28	22	40	*	*	8	1	1
1979	100	26	25	39	1	*	6	1	1

* Not applicable   —(¹) Less than ½ per cent.

Percentage of persons aged 17 and under 21 sentenced for indictable/triable-either-way offences who received various sentences by sex and type of sentence or order

England and Wales

Sex and year	Total	Absolute or conditional discharge	Probation order	Fine	Community service order	Detention centre order	Borstal training	Imprisonment Suspended	Imprisonment Immediate	Otherwise dealt with
Males					Indictable offences					
1969	100	9	14	53	*	8	8	4	3	2
1970	100	8	12	54	*	9	8	3	3	2
1971	100	8	12	54	*	8	8	3	3	3
1972	100	8	12	55	*	8	7	4	4	2
1973	100	8	11	59	*	6	7	3	3	3
1974	100	7	10	60	1	6	7	3	3	2
1975	100	8	9	59	2	6	7	4	3	2
1976	100	8	8	57	4	6	7	4	5	2
1977	100	8	7	57	5	6	6	4	5	2
1978	100	7	6	57	6	6	6	4	5	2
					Indictable/triable-either-way offences					
1977	100	7	7	55	6	6	7	4	5	2
1978	100	6	7	55	7	6	7	5	6	2
1979	100	6	7	54	7	6	6	5	6	2
Females					Indictable offences					
1969	100	20	32	41	*	*	3	2	1	1
1970	100	19	29	45	*	*	3	2	1	1
1971	100	20	28	46	*	*	3	2	1	1
1972	100	20	26	48	*	*	2	3	1	1
1973	100	19	24	51	*	*	2	2	1	1
1974	100	19	23	52	*	*	2	2	1	1
1975	100	20	22	51	(¹)	*	3	2	1	2
1976	100	20	20	51	(¹)	*	2	3	1	1
1977	100	20	19	52	1	*	2	3	1	1
1978	100	18	18	53	2	*	2	4	2	1
					Indictable/triable-either-way offences					
1977	100	20	19	52	2	*	2	3	1	1
1978	100	17	18	54	2	*	2	4	2	2
1979	100	17	19	52	2	*	2	4	2	1

Percentage of total persons sentenced

* Not applicable   (¹) Less than ½ per cent.

89

APPENDIX III: CAUTIONING RATES

Offenders cautioned by type of offence, sex and age

England and Wales 1979

Number of offenders

Type of offence	Males				Females			
	All ages	Aged 10 and under 14	Aged 14 and under 17	Aged 17 and under 21	All ages	Aged 10 and under 14	Aged 14 and under 17	Aged 17 and under 21
Indictable/triable-either-way offences								
Violence against the person	3,682	841	1,618	279	978	187	454	76
Sexual offences	2,781	294	1,015	927	61	11	13	10
Burglary	9,147	5,074	3,795	182	828	442	332	29
Robbery	88	53	31	2	11	2	9	–
Theft and handling stolen goods	49,853	23,619	21,245	1,464	25,075	11,140	9,213	527
Fraud and forgery	829	215	357	52	397	68	142	46
Criminal damage	1,860	1,032	734	51	163	87	58	5
Other (excluding motoring offences)	906	20	89	63	122	3	30	23
Total	69,146	31,148	28,884	3,020	27,635	11,940	10,251	716
Summary offences (excluding motoring offences)								
Total	30,239	5,148	9,503	3,154	9,479	375	977	2,860
All offences (excluding motoring offences)								
Total	99,385	36,296	38,387	6,174	37,114	12,315	11,228	3,576

Males aged 10 and under 17 cautioned as a percentage of males aged 10 and under 17 found guilty or cautioned by police force area and offence group[1]

England and Wales 1979

Percentage of males found guilty or cautioned

Police force area	Total indictable/ triable-either-way offences	Violence against the person	Burglary	Theft and handling stolen goods	Summary offences (excluding motoring offences)
Avon and Somerset	43	24	28	51	45
Bedfordshire	49	36	24	58	43
Cambridgeshire	43	(43)	31	48	47
Cheshire	45	24	25	57	23
Cleveland	36	33	16	46	35
Cumbria	43	(17)	23	54	37
Derbyshire	43	28	28	53	41
Devon and Cornwall	61	50	38	69	64
Dorset	60	(47)	28	67	52
Durham	45	38	30	48	10
Essex	54	39	41	61	67
Gloucestershire	46	(28)	17	56	45
Greater Manchester	37	13	22	45	9
Hampshire	59	28	44	67	57
Hertfordshire	46	15	20	52	5
Humberside	30	29	18	35	44
Kent	48	47	32	56	53
Lancashire	49	32	31	60	45
Leicestershire	47	28	33	55	56
Lincolnshire	58	(39)	40	67	50

Merseyside	39	22	24	48	46
Metropolitan Police District(2)	44	32	30	50	41
Norfolk	46	(24)	35	54	8
Northamptonshire	41	(20)	28	45	15
Northumbria	47	29	29	57	43
North Yorkshire	43	(24)	21	52	32
Nottinghamshire	52	44	31	61	50
South Yorkshire	39	26	26	46	40
Staffordshire	50	37	32	62	34
Suffolk	63	(41)	44	72	64
Surrey	50	(29)	30	62	58
Sussex	52	45	31	62	42
Thames Valley	47	19	31	58	49
Warwickshire	44	(25)	29	52	42
West Mercia	57	37	43	68	49
West Midlands	48	26	36	57	38
West Yorkshire	42	33	25	51	44
Wiltshire	52	(32)	37	61	26
England	46	30	29	54	42
Dyfed-Powys	67	(32)	59	74	64
Gwent	42	(33)	25	50	51
North Wales	44	(33)	34	52	51
South Wales	28	10	16	37	24
Wales	38	22	26	46	41
England and Wales	45	30	29	54	42

(1) Separate percentages have not been given for the other offence groups because the number of males aged 10 and under 17 found guilty of or cautioned for those offences in each police force area is too small for meaningful comparisons to be made.

(2) Including City of London

( ) Percentage based on less than 100 persons and therefore subject to wide variation.

92

Females aged 10 and under 17 cautioned as a percentage of females aged 10 and under 17 found guilty or cautioned by police force area and offence group([1])

England and Wales 1979   Percentage of females found guilty or cautioned

Police force area	Total indictable/ triable-either- way offences	Theft and handling stolen goods
Avon and Somerset	66	72
Bedfordshire	71	73
Cambridgeshire	51	54
Cheshire	73	79
Cleveland	70	74
Cumbria	71	72
Derbyshire	64	66
Devon and Cornwall	80	83
Dorset	75	79
Durham	74	79
Essex	81	84
Gloucestershire	62	69
Greater Manchester	68	73
Hampshire	83	86
Hertfordshire	78	82
Humberside	48	51
Kent	72	76
Lancashire	76	81
Leicestershire	67	71
Lincolnshire	72	78
Merseyside	73	76
Metropolitan Police District([2])	66	70
Norfolk	78	80
Northamptonshire	65	70
Northumbria	76	81
North Yorkshire	62	66
Nottinghamshire	76	81
South Yorkshire	63	65
Staffordshire	74	79
Suffolk	89	91
Surrey	70	83
Sussex	64	68
Thames Valley	69	74
Warwickshire	65	66
West Mercia	78	82
West Midlands	79	82
West Yorkshire	66	72
Wiltshire	75	79
England	71	75
Dyfed-Powys	78	82
Gwent	55	56
North Wales	68	74
South Wales	66	72
Wales	65	69
England and Wales	71	75

([1]) Separate percentages have not been given for the other offence groups because the number of females aged 10 and under 17 found guilty of or cautioned for those offences in each police force area is too small for meaningful comparisons to be made.
([2]) Including City of London

93

The working party has received an impressive volume of evidence describing the operation of intermediate treatment schemes in several areas of the country. This appendix describes four schemes about which we have received particularly full information. The Director of 870 House, Birmingham, addressed a recent meeting of the Parliamentary All-Party Penal Affairs Group about the work of his unit; a member of our working party, Baroness Faithfull, provided us with detailed information about the work of the Pontefract Activity Centre; and members of the working party visited the Green Lanes Intermediate Treatment Centre, Haringey, and the Medway Close Support Unit in the course of our enquiry.

The Green Lanes Centre

The Green Lanes Intermediate Treatment Centre, Haringey, was established early in 1978 to cater for delinquents aged 15 to 18 who would otherwise be placed in residential care. It consists of two large houses converted into a single unit and providing educational and meeting rooms, a games room, office space, kitchen and a garden in which a workshop has been built. The project is staffed by four full time intermediate treatment workers and one full time and two part time teachers.

The majority of referrals come from social workers and probation officers. Once referred, the young person meets project staff for mutual assessment, after which a contract is negotiated with the young person, project workers, and where possible the family, social worker, probation officer, school or employer. This involves the project worker in proposing a systematic programme which will last for a six, nine or twelve month period. A report is then prepared which puts the proposed plan before the court and requests the opportunity to carry it out, usually in conjunction with a supervision order.

The project provides programmes which involve some or all of the following:

(a)   education, which is mainly in numeracy and literacy and also includes assistance in following specialist educational projects of the child's own choice.

(b)   workshops and work training, which aim to familiarise young people with equipment and skills so that they can go on to further education and training, or to give them enough confidence and experience to compete more successfully in the job market. The project possesses two workshops, one offering woodwork and metalwork and another equipped as a motor vehicle workshop. (The latter workshop also provides the headquarters of a separately managed banger racing project). Other options included electronics, bricklaying, painting and decorating, welding and typing.

(c)   work experience, run in collaboration with the careers service, which provides experience two days a week with a local business or other organisation. Work experience placements encompass building work, painting and decorating, retail trades, light engineering, old people's homes, advice centres, a centre for the mentally handicapped and a riding stable for handicapped children.

(d)   accommodation, which is provided by means of a separately managed scheme providing accommodation for homeless young people.

(e)   advice and counselling, both individually and in groups.

During the scheme's first three operational years, the number of those attending the centre who reoffended, either while participating in the project or afterwards while still of juvenile age, was around 25 per cent.

870 House

870 House is based in a large three-storey house in the Selly Oak area of Birmingham. It caters for children aged 8 to 18, the majority being in the 12-16 age range. The unit operates 24 hours a day, seven days a week, and employs five methods which are used separately or jointly as appropriate to the individual child's needs. These are:

(a)   individual counselling and casework.

(b)   groups where individual and group problems are identified and discussed.

(c)   activity groups, where members are encouraged to develop skills with a view to their gaining self-confidence and a sense of achievement. These include carpentry, painting and decorating, sewing, silk screen printing, motor mechanics, drama, art, pottery and sporting and recreational activities.

(d)   remedial work, wnere members are helped with specific problems such as educational difficulties and employment problems. The unit provides full time educational services for children who have been suspended from school or cannot attend school for some other reason, a "bussing" service taking persistent non-attenders to school each day, a remedial education service providing help in literacy and numeracy, a job guidance service, and job experience and support for long term unemployed youth.

(e)   community work, tackling problems in the local community including housing conditions, lack of facilities or peer group activities which appear to contribute significantly to the child's problem.

The unit also provides part time residential care facilities, family casework and a visiting service which can be available at times such as mealtimes, bedtimes and the crucial time when children are due to leave for school or work. Holiday schemes are run throughout the school holidays and a series of camps are provided in the summer holidays. The unit has three full time staff and 27 part time volunteers: over half the latter are in fact professionally qualified.

The proportion of young people attending who are subject to supervision and care orders is about 40 per cent, and a further 20-25 per cent are referred by the police. The extent of children's involvement with the unit varies: some spend most of their waking hours with the unit, while others attend two or three times a week. 34 per cent of the attenders reoffend within two years, and over an eight year period only 5 per cent have subsequently entered residential establishments.

The Pontefract Activity Centre

The Pontefract Activity Centre aims to avoid inappropriate residential care and to reduce the level of delinquency by fostering a positive relationship between young people and their community. The Centre is based in a prefabricated two-storey building with a workshop area, gym, garage and mechanics area, indoor activity area and several smaller discussion rooms. It has been managed by Barnardo's since 1974 and has a local Advisory Panel which includes representatives of local agencies concerned with young people: its tasks include support and advice to staff, liaison with local professionals and the community, and fund raising responsibilities. The Centre has five full time staff and the services of teachers and youth leaders on a sessional basis, and it also makes considerable use of volunteers. In any one term it works with 170 children, with a core group of about 50. Some are referred by local agencies, but the centre has an open door policy and many are self-referrals.

The Centre is open five days a week from 9a.m. to 9p.m. and some weekends, and its methods consist of individual and family social work, community work, informal and intensive work with groups and education. A drop-in advice facility is also available. Group work includes outdoor pursuits and regular evening activities and group discussion. School holidays provide an opportunity to work with groups during the day on the upkeep and decoration of the building, the conservation of land adjoining the building and community projects. A recent extension of the project has been into intensive day time work with a small group of those offending or considered to be at risk of offending as a result of their school-based problems or unemployment. Early results are positive.

The project's community work involves initiating and supporting projects aimed at areas of need identified by the young people themselves as being linked with the causes of their delinquency. For example, a group of young people from a particular estate claimed in discussion groups that lack of facilities on their estate was an important factor in their getting into trouble. The project workers asked the community constable to introduce them to adults on the estate who had complained to him about the local children and to any others who might be interested in helping. This group then formed a community association with a youth committee attached. Within a few months they had raised a considerable amount of money and found a burned out prefabricated house ten miles away which the Housing Department donated. Project workers, children and parents helped to dismantle and transport the prefabricated sections and, using the Centre's workshop, worked to rebuild the building as a community centre.

The Centre's work is considered by the local authority to have been an important factor in reducing the demand for residential care for juveniles in the area.

The Medway Close Support Unit
The Medway Close Support Unit, which was opened in 1979, is a joint venture managed by the Kent Probation and After-Care Service and funded by the Kent Social Services Department. It provides a form of intensive intermediate treatment for up to twelve children aged 14 to 16, who have appeared before the juvenile court charged with offences which would normally attract a custodial sentence, and is staffed with a probation officer, two supervisors and a unit parent.

Children attend the Unit for a fourteen week period. It provides twelve hours supervision a day from Monday to Friday and involvement in a task of value to the community from 9a.m. to 4p.m. on Saturdays. Trainees leave home in the morning to attend school or work, where their attendance is monitored by telephone calls from Unit staff and immediate action is taken if the trainee defaults. If these normal activities cannot be or are not being pursued during the day, the trainee attends the Probation Service's day centre which is housed in the same building as the Close Support Unit.

At the end of the school or working day, trainees make their way to the Close Support Unit, where they have a meal. During the evening any trainee engaged in a positive evening activity before entering the Unit is encouraged to continue this and any trainee who needs to study or pursue homework is given appropriate guidance to do so. For all other trainees, the evening period is occupied until 8.30p.m. with positive activities including handicraft and sport, either within the Unit or in supervised excursions outside the Unit. At 8.30p.m. trainees leave the Unit and make their way home. The staff carry out spot checks until 10p.m. to ensure that trainees arrive home within a reasonable time and to maintain liaison with the family and home. On Saturdays the trainees pursue work of value to the community and supervised leisure pursuits under the supervision of selected sessional supervisors.

The Unit works with parents, enabling them to set realistic standards. Its counselling and support has clearly enabled many parents to deal with situations more confidently and helped to establish norms that are acceptable both within the home and at the Unit.

50 trainees were accepted into the Unit between February 1979 and December 1980, of whom two failed to complete the required period at the Unit and were taken into residential care. Of the remaining 48 trainees, 38 had completed the required period in December 1980 and ten were currently attending the Unit. Ten of the trainees had committed offences while attending the Unit (half of which were committed in one incident discovered by Unit staff and reported to the police, which would not otherwise have come to police notice).

APPENDIX V: ORGANISATIONS AND INDIVIDUALS WHO SUBMITTED EVIDENCE TO THE WORKING PARTY

Apex Trust
Association of Chief Police Officers
Association of Community Homes
Association of County Councils
Association of Directors of Social Services
Association of Metropolitan Authorities
Bayswater Centre, Bristol
British Association of Social Workers
Mr Malcolm Bryant
Ms Pam Burns
Centre of Youth, Crime and Community, University of Lancaster
Church of England Children's Society
Mr J. Clulee
Commission for Racial Equality
Conference of Chief Probation Officers
Ms Coline Covington
Croydon Guild of Voluntary Organisations
Department of Health and Social Security
Mrs Barbara Dyer
870 House, Birmingham
Fabian Society
Ms Betty Farrar
Federation of Alcoholic Residential Establishments
Green Lanes Intermediate Treatment Centre, Haringey
Mr John Harding
Mr Brian Harris
Mr Maurice Hawker
Miss Nancy Hazel
Miss Sheila Himmel
Mr Derek Hollamby
Mr Christopher Holtom
Home Office
Howard League for Penal Reform
Ms Valerie Howarth
Mr Philip Hughes

Hyper-Active Children's Support Group
Justice for Children
Justices' Clerks' Society
Kent Family Project
Dr Gerry Lawton
Mr B. Lilley
Ms Kirstie Maclean
Magistrates' Association
Medway Close Support Unit
Mr George T. Meredith
Mrs Helen Miller
Mr Spencer Millham
National Association for the Care and Resettlement of Offenders
National Association of Probation Officers
National Council for Civil Liberties
National Council for Voluntary Organisations
National Youth Bureau
New Approaches to Juvenile Crime
New Careers Project, Bristol
Dr Margaret Norris
Northern Ireland Office
Police Federation of England and Wales
Police Superintendents' Association of England and Wales
Pontefract Activity Centre
POP Workshops, Staines
Prison and Borstal Governors' Branch, Society of Civil and Public Servants
Prison Officers' Association
Rainer Foundation
Mr Peter Ralphs
Mr Ian Reid
Mrs Mary Reinach
Residential Care Association
Mrs Margaret Richardson J.P.
Social Workers' Group, Tameside
Mr Nicolas Stacey
Standing Conference on Drug Abuse
Mrs Joanna Staughton J.P.

Mr S.C. Trotter
Mr R.C. Tweed
Mr R. Vaughan-Jones
Yorkshire and Humberside Intermediate Treatment Association
Youthaid